ENTERING THE KINGDOM
THE PATHWAY TO GOD'S KINGDOM
THROUGH THE BOOK OF ACTS

JOE FERRAGAMO SR.

CONTENTS

Praise for Entering the Kingdom	vii
Foreword	ix
Foreword	xi
Introduction	xv
1. The Kingdom of God	1
2. Ye Shall Receive Power	19
3. What Meaneth This?	39
4. Peter's First Gospel Sermon	61
5. They Continued	79
6. Before the Jewish Council	95
7. On To the Gentiles	117
8. An About-Face	133
9. The Gospel to Samaria	151
10. Chapter 29	173
11. The End of the Age	195
12. God's Glorious Kingdom	211
Acknowledgments	219
End Notes	221

ENTERING THE KINGDOM
By Joseph Ferragamo Sr.

Published by Late November Literary
Winston Salem, NC 27107

ISBN (Print): 978-1-7375561-7-6
Copyright 2023 by Joe Ferragamo
Cover design by Sweet N' Spicy designs
Interior design by Late November Literary

Available in print or online. Visit latenovemberliterary.com or josephferragamo.com.

All rights reserved. No part of this publication may be reproduced in any form without written permission of the publisher, except as provided by the U.S. copyright law.

All Scriptures are taken from the Holy Bible, King James Version (Public Domain), unless otherwise documented and cited.

Library of Congress Cataloging-in-Publication data

Ferragamo Sr., Joseph.

Entering the Kingdom / Joseph Ferragamo Sr. 1st ed.

Printed in the United States of America

This book is dedicated to my Father and Mother who, from my childhood, instilled in me a love and reverence for God and to my brother Ralph who was the one who led me and my wife into the Kingdom of God.

PRAISE FOR ENTERING THE KINGDOM

I have just finished reading, *Entering The Kingdom,* by Joseph Ferragamo. Rev. Ferragamo has given sincere believers thorough and thoughtful insight into the Kingdom of God through the Book of Acts. I appreciate the way this book dispels some of the myths and the mysteries surrounding the work of the Holy Spirit in the New Testament church, and in the global church in our day. Entering The Kingdom is a great resource for anyone hungry and thirsty for a genuine, supernatural, and Bible based, experience with God. I highly recommend this book and intend to share this book with Christians that are longing for more of God.

~Rev. Harold Linder, pastor at Heavenview UPC

FOREWORD

I highly recommend that you prayerfully read and study "ENTERING THE KINGDOM." From the moment that I started reading this book, I was gripped by its insight into God's Holy Word. Its pages contain DIVINE INSIGHT for our world that is spinning out of control because mankind has more interest in the earthly kingdom than in the heavenly kingdom. Consequently, our nation has lost its way and we are stumbling like blind beggars down the broad way that leads to destruction.

The author, Joe Ferragamo, and his wife, Barbara, experienced the outpouring of the supernatural in their lives in 1975 that totally turned them around. Their lifestyle immediately changed. I was privileged to have a front-row seat as their first pastor in Queens, NY, and watch as the Almighty grafted HIS NATURE into their hearts and their everyday lives. I will never forget the night they called me and said, "Pastor listen" – I heard the sound of running water and then joyful laughter – they asked, "do you know what is happening?" I didn't know. So, they begin to explain - - we are flushing all of our liquor down the toilet. That night, they were high on the New Wine.

For nearly fifty years Joe has been an avid student of the Bible. He has researched history and numerous commentaries of the Bible. He has diligently fulfilled 2 Tim 2:15, "Study to shew thyself approved unto God, a workman that needeth not to be ashamed, rightly dividing the word of truth." Rest assured, that in the reading of *ENTERING THE KINGDOM*, Joe has carefully followed Isaiah 28:13, making sure that precept is upon precept and line is upon line. This book is PROFOUND – it has Biblical depth and accuracy yet is SIMPLE – easy to comprehend. Read, study, and enjoy and then experience the beautiful experience of the infilling of the Holy Ghost.

~Rev. Gerald D. Morris

FOREWORD

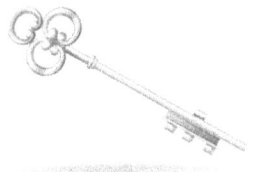

In his book, "Entering the Kingdom," author Joseph Ferragamo, examines the most important subject that can ever be considered by mankind; the eternal destiny of the human soul.

Jesus frequently referenced the Kingdom of God, (the Kingdom of Heaven) during His earthly ministry. So fundamental is this subject that Jesus called His message "the gospel of the Kingdom" and declared that it would be preached throughout the whole world. He further emphasized its importance in Luke 13:24 by instructing His followers to "strive to enter in" denoting that human effort was involved in the process.

Understanding the significance of "The Kingdom" and how to gain entrance into it, is the centric doctrine of Christianity. And these are the themes Ferragamo thoughtfully addresses in this book.

Weaving together a three-fold-cord of personal experiences, scholarly resources, and scriptural evidence, Ferragamo constructs a powerful and compelling apologetic for the original "gospel of the kingdom" that was introduced by John the Baptist, reiterated by Jesus Christ, and "unlocked" by the Apostle Peter on the Day of Pentecost.

Not only is this book a "good read," it serves an important practical purpose, providing valuable insight on how any individual can be successful in the most important goal of life, "Entering The Kingdom."

~Rev. Doug Davis, Jr.

But covet earnestly the best gifts: and yet shew I unto you *a more excellent way*.
~1 Corinthians 12:31~

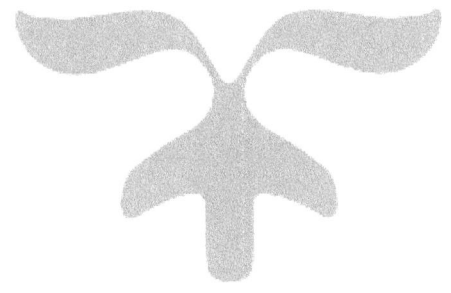

INTRODUCTION

Heaven! Many books have been written about this beautiful place where the throne of the One Holy, True God exists. How do we know about this place? How can we know what awaits us when we arrive there? What will it be like when we first enter through those pearly gates? What will we do there? Will we be just spiritual beings floating around with no bodies? What will it be like to see God?

These and many other questions have filled my mind since I was a young boy. I was born into an Italian Catholic family. My father and mother were good Catholics that went to Sunday Mass just about every week as long as they were not ill. I attribute my love for God to my parents who reared me in the fear and admonition of the Lord. After Sunday Mass, my father would always preach another sermon based upon what he heard in church that morning.

When I was eight years old, I desired to become a priest. I would go to Mass every day during the summer and sit in the first pew, my eyes so attentive to what the priest was doing. I daydreamed often about being on that altar area and performing the ritual that the priests did during the Mass. I felt it was the closest place on earth to being in God's presence. Heaven wasn't a new concept for me at that point.

Even back then, I longed for heaven. Heaven was where I wanted to be, and Heaven is where I want to go even today.

As I grew, my hopes of becoming a priest were dashed because I did so poorly on my high school entrance exams that I was not allowed to go to the high school preparatory seminary that would have prepared me for an actual seminary. I served as an altar boy into my sophomore year in high school but after realizing that I would never be able to follow my dream to be a priest I shifted my attention to playing sports and dating girls. In 1969 I met a beautiful, sensitive young girl who would later become my precious, loving, and loyal wife and soulmate. Together we continued to observe the Sunday devotions and special services in the Catholic Church.

After two years my wife gave birth to our first child, a boy. As all good Catholics (and even some not so good ones) do, we set out to have our child Christened, which is the way Catholic's baptize. I asked my brother to be my boy's godfather. About two weeks before the ceremony, my brother called to tell me that he couldn't go ahead with the plan to be my child's godfather. My wife and I were a bit confused because my brother mentioned something about having an experience with God that is found in the Bible. Although he couldn't join in the ceremony, he said he would attend the party. That's when both my wife's and my attention was piqued.

God had blessed us with a beautiful day. We had an outdoor party in our backyard for my son's "baptism." When my brother entered the yard my wife and I looked at each other because we were both thinking the same thing. "What had happened to him?" His face seemed to shine! After the party was over my brother began to tell us of his experience. He said that he was filled with the Holy Ghost just like the Apostles were on the Day of Pentecost. He talked of a Pentecostal experience where he spoke in other tongues as he was filled with the Holy Ghost.

Now because I had studied well in my religion classes, I knew about what happened on Pentecost Sunday, but this was the first time I had ever heard of this happening in our day. Although the Catholic

Church spoke about Pentecost Sunday, they never even hinted that we could actually have that same Pentecostal experience today. I had read that the Apostles spoke in tongues, but I had no clue as to what that meant. It was all a mystery to me. My wife and I were extremely interested since we had recently stopped going to church and had been thinking about dabbling into some curious arts like reading tarot cards and white witchcraft. We attended our first Pentecostal Church service in 1975 in Schenectady NY, which was about 250 miles from where we lived in Queens, NY. The service seemed normal to us. There was much singing and worship and then the Word of God was preached. After the preaching, the minister called the people forward and that is when my wife and I were a bit startled. Many of the people went to the altar area and began to pray out loud. My wife and I both started to feel something, and we were frightened. They were so exuberant and passionate that it scared the both of us, and we ran out of the church. Coming from Catholic Church where you are told as a child to be quiet in church, Pentecostal worship is loud and demonstrative. My brother came out to look for us, and he brought us back in assuring us that no one would harm us and that what we felt was the presence of the Lord.

Though we were frightened we did go back into the church. A man gave us both a bible and he told us that God had put a seed in our heart and that we should allow it to grow. Our first experience with Pentecost left us with an intense desire to know more so we started reading the Bible at night before going to bed. We started reading in the Book of Matthew. One night after reading that Jesus cast out a devil, I waxed bold and rebuked the devil too. Instantly the window shade in our bedroom flew up to the top and twirled around a few times. We were extremely frightened, but we made up our minds right then that we would return to the Pentecostal Church and would receive the Holy Ghost. On September 23, 1975, both my wife and I received the Holy Ghost as we spoke in a language we had never learned and were baptized in the only name under heaven, given among men, whereby we must be saved: the Name of Jesus.

When we returned home from upstate New York, we took all of our liquor bottles we had in the house, including new unopened bottles we bought for our baby's christening, and we dumped them all down the drain in the sink. We were laughing and singing as we did so. That was the beginning of our Pentecostal experience, and we are both still serving the Lord 47 years later.

God's Spirit: Heaven on Earth

Receiving God's Spirit was the greatest day of my life and His Spirit is the greatest gift anyone has ever given to me. I cherish His Spirit with all my heart.

So, what is Heaven? Heaven is the place of God's throne (*Matthew 5:34; Acts 7:49*), and Heaven is where God is (*Matthew 5:16, 45; 6:9; 16:17*). Heaven will be paradise because Heaven will be eternity with the Lord. Through the years of learning and growing in God, I've discovered that the road to Heaven is a journey. As it is with any journey from point A to point B, we usually need a road map. Our journey from here to Heaven is no different. The road map God gave us is His Divine Word; the Bible. Unlike our world's view that there are many roads that lead to Heaven, the Bible teaches us that there is only one road, one way.

> *You can enter God's Kingdom only through the narrow gate. The highway to hell is broad, and its gate is wide for the many who choose that way. But the gateway to life is very narrow and the road is difficult, and only a few ever find it. (Matthew 7:13-14 NLT)*

> *Jesus saith unto him, I am the way, the truth, and the life: no man cometh unto the Father, but by me. (John 14:6)*

The Bible also talks about a Kingdom, God's Kingdom. God's Kingdom was in eternity past where God exercised His right to rule over all things. His Kingdom will one day fill the earth, when He reigns in glory during the Millennial Reign of Jesus Christ following the Battle of Armageddon. The Bible tells us that there is a way for us to enter into the Kingdom of God today. We find this in John Chapter 3 when Jesus is talking with Nicodemus:

> *Jesus answered and said unto him, Verily, verily, I say unto thee, Except a man be born again, he cannot see the kingdom of God. Nicodemus saith unto him, How can a man be born when he is old? can he enter the second time into his mother's womb, and be born? Jesus answered, Verily, verily, I say unto thee, Except a man be born of water and of the Spirit, he cannot enter into the kingdom of God. That which is born of the flesh is flesh; and that which is born of the Spirit is spirit. Marvel not that I said unto thee, Ye must be born again. (John 3:3-7)*

This is what it means to be "born again." Jesus told Nicodemus that he *must* be born again if he wanted to see the Kingdom of God. You must be born of water and the Spirit, that is water baptism in the Name of Jesus Christ for the remission of sins and being filled with the gift of the Holy Ghost, speaking in other tongues as the Spirit gives the utterance, if you want to enter the Kingdom of God.

A More Perfect Way

Now I realize that this may not be your experience at this point in your walk with the Lord. Please understand that I am not trying to take away anything that you have received from God. Whatever it is that God has given to you, hold on to it and don't let it go. But what if there's more? Think of children on Christmas morning. What if they opened one gift while several more lay under the tree.

"Aren't you going to open the rest of your gifts?" A parent might ask.

"No, I'm fine with just this one."

For most of our children, this would never happen. There is such joy in the giving and receiving of gifts. Children can't wait to open up all of their Christmas gifts.

The same is true in growing our relationship with Christ. What if there are more presents under the Christmas tree? Does it make sense to walk away, knowing that God has so much more for us? In the New Testament there is a brief story about a man named Apollos in Acts chapter 18. The scripture says that Apollos was, "an eloquent man, and mighty in the scriptures." He was a follower of John the Baptist and was only introduced to John's baptism. There were a couple in the church named Aquilla and Priscilla, and when they heard him speak so boldly in the synagogue, they took him and began to show him the way of God more perfectly.

This is what this book endeavors to do. My early years in the Catholic church were just the beginning of my walk with the Lord. Even then, He was drawing me to Him and to truly receive all that He had for me. Whatever your experience is with God, I hope to show you what I've learned through the years: that there is so much more for you to receive, if you will only open your heart to God in faith. If you desire to grow in your relationship with God, and as Philippians 3:10 says, to truly know Him "in the power of His resurrection," please read on.

1
THE KINGDOM OF GOD

When I was a young boy, we used to play a game called King of the Hill. Someone would start by taking his place on top of the hill as king. The rest of us would try our best to push, wrestle, or do anything we could to make the king fall. The person who was able to dethrone the king then became the new king. The game would go on until either we got tired of the game, or someone was so strong or heavy that we couldn't knock him off of his throne.

This is the essence of war. Kingdoms fight against kingdoms to become the strongest and most powerful in the world. From the beginning of time men have fought many battles with the expectation that they would emerge as the greatest kingdom on earth, only to be challenged by some other nation in the future.

This is something not only seen in physical kingdoms, but also in spiritual ones. The greatest battle between spiritual kingdoms is the one between the Kingdom of Almighty God and the kingdom of Satan. God has a Kingdom, and He rules from heaven and has all authority in this Kingdom. By the same token, Satan also has dominion over his own kingdom on the earth, from which he rules and continually fights against the Kingdom of God. These two kingdoms exist side by side and the battle is a daily one for the souls of men and women all over the earth!

The Kingdom of God Defined

To define the Kingdom of God, we must first understand who He is and why His Kingdom matters. God is a being like no other. He has no equals and He has no opposites. Satan is NOT God's opposite, because satan is not a viable opponent since God created him and gave him is power.

God is an eternal being, meaning He never had a beginning and He will never have an ending. That is something our finite minds cannot fully comprehend. God is the very essence of holiness, and He is above all of His creation. He is all-powerful, all knowing, and He is everywhere all at the same time. That is why the psalmist wrote this in the 139th Psalm:

> *I can never escape from your Spirit! I can never get away from your presence! If I go up to heaven, you are there; if I go down to the grave, you are there. If I ride the wings of the morning, if I dwell by the farthest oceans, even there your hand will guide me, and your strength will support me. (Psalm 139:7-10 NLT)*

Even in all His greatness, He is a personal God and He desires to have a relationship with you and me. His nature is Love and He is so good, merciful, compassionate, and He has prepared a beautiful place for us to live together with Him throughout all eternity.

God is also a King! The Bible calls Jesus the "King of Kings" (*Revelation 19:16*) for He is greater than any other king that has ever reigned or ever will reign. As a King, God has a Kingdom. His Kingdom is the realm from which He sovereignly rules, reigns, and has total authority. The subject of God's Kingdom is so vast that it can be found in the Bible from Genesis to Revelation.

That's why in the introduction to his book, J. Dwight Pentecost described the Kingdom of God in this way:

The great theme of God's kingdom program can be found throughout the Bible, from Genesis to Revelation. It is a theme that unifies all of Scripture. Through it the Bible records the progressive unfolding of a program in which God reveals His sovereign authority. And through it God demonstrates His right to rule through various forms of a kingdom He establishes here on earth, beginning in Genesis and consummating in the reign of Jesus Christ as King of kings and Lord of lords in the Book of Revelation. [1]

In these last days, we need to pray and ask God to anoint our eyes. His miraculous works are all around us. Let us not turn a blind eye to them. But as it was on the Day of Pentecost, so it is today. When speaking of God's miraculous outpouring of His Holy Spirit, some are amazed and desire to receive it, but some mockingly say, "What Meaneth This?"

The Kingdom of God is basically the rule of God. It is God's reign, the divine sovereignty in action. God's reign, however, is manifested in several realms, and the Gospels speak of entering into the Kingdom of God both today and tomorrow. God's reign manifests itself both in the future and in the present and thereby creates both a future realm and a present realm in which man may experience the blessings of His reign. [2]

You may ask: does the Kingdom of God refer to things happening now and things happening in the future? Yes! For instance, when the Pharisees wanted to know when God's Kingdom would come:

He (Jesus) answered them and said, The kingdom of God cometh not with observation: Neither shall they say, Lo here! or, lo there! for, behold, the kingdom of God is within you. (Luke 17:20-21)

Jesus was saying that His Kingdom would not be found by visible signs; there would be no visible display, but the Kingdom of God is within you, within your heart, or already among you. In fact, the King of the Kingdom stood right in front of those Pharisees and yet they couldn't see Him nor could they understand His Words.

> *The word 'observation' means 'to watch carefully'... Jesus meant that the future earthly kingdom would not come slowly as a political movement which could be seen to evolve (compare John 18:36).* [3]

Jesus also said:

> "The law and the prophets were until John: since that time the kingdom of God is preached, and every man presseth into it. (Luke 16:16)

> And he sent them to preach the kingdom of God, and to heal the sick. (Luke 9:2)

Jesus did speak as though His Kingdom was present with us but then there were times when Jesus spoke of the Kingdom as something future:

> *But I tell you of a truth, there be some standing here, which shall not taste of death, till they see the kingdom of God. (Luke 9:27)*

> *For I say unto you, I will not drink of the fruit of the vine, until the kingdom of God shall come. (Luke 22:18)*

The Apostle Paul weighs in with his own thought on the subject:

> *Now this I say, brethren, that flesh and blood cannot inherit the kingdom of God; neither doth corruption inherit incorruption.*
> *(1 Corinthians 15:50).*

It seems from these verses that the Kingdom can be both present and future, and that the Kingdom must be inherited through specific actions. Yes, we must be born into the Kingdom of God according to the biblical account found in John's Gospel (*John 3:3,5*). And as children of God, we will receive a wonderful inheritance that is waiting for us in the heavens.

> *The Spirit Himself [thus] testifies together with our own spirit, [assuring us] that we are children of God. And if we are [His] children, then we are [His] heirs also: heirs of God and fellow heirs with Christ [sharing His inheritance with Him]; only we must share His suffering if we are to share His glory. (Romans 8:16-17 AMP)*

The Fall of Lucifer

In the beginning God ruled in the heavens before the creation of heaven and earth. This is sometimes spoken of as God ruling in "eternity past." During this time, it is believed, that God created the heavenly host of angels. They were created to worship God and to be His messengers to His "earthly" servants. The most beautiful angel of all God's creation was Lucifer. He had a special place in God's creation. He was full of wisdom and beauty and was the highest of all the created beings. He was responsible for leading the worship of God and he was present in Eden, the Garden of God (*Ezekiel 28:13*).

He also was an anointed cherub, guarding the glory of God (*Ezekiel 28:14*). He was perfect in all his ways until iniquity was found in him (*Ezekiel 28:15*). His pride caused him to rebel against God and in the process, Lucifer caused one-third of the angels of heaven to follow after him. They were all cast out of heaven and Lucifer, now referred to as Satan, has set up his kingdom on the earth. Since that time there has been conflict between the Kingdom of God and the counterfeit kingdom of Satan. There will be conflict between these kingdoms as Satan continually opposes God from establishing His Kingdom on the earth and this will continue until Satan is cast into the lake of fire at the end of time, which is the beginning of eternity!

When did the fall of Satan occur? Actually, the Bible isn't clear as to when it happened. There are those who believe that it happened before God created the heaven and the earth, in eternity past. I tend to disagree with them because, when God finished creating, He looked at His creation and said that it was "very good" (*Genesis 1:31*). If Satan had already rebelled against God, he would have been cast out of heaven and his kingdom would have infected the earth with sin. How then could God say that all His creation was "very good?"

Creation And the Fall of Man

So, God created the heavens and the earth (*Genesis 1:1*). He created the expanse of the heavens, the sun, moon, and stars. He created the galaxies of the universe, so vast that scientists say that the universe keeps expanding all the time. He created the dry land and the seas (*Genesis 1:9-13*). He created the birds of the air, the fish in the sea, and all the animals, and all the creeping things in the earth (*Genesis 1:20-21, 24-25*). Then as a last climactic work, God created man in His image, after His likeness (*Genesis 1:26-27*). God then gave to man the privilege to rule and have dominion over all His creation. God blessed the man and placed him in a beautiful garden, a special place prepared by God, so that the man could exercise the dominion given to him. His authority would be over all of God's new creation: the birds, fish, animals and creeping things.

> *And God blessed them, and God said unto them, Be fruitful, and multiply, and replenish the earth, and subdue it: and have dominion over the fish of the sea, and over the fowl of the air, and over every living thing that moveth upon the earth. (Genesis 1:28)*

God gave man dominion and the right to rule His Kingdom under His guidance as His representative while Adam and Eve were in the Garden of Eden. As Pentecost explains it: "He [man] would establish a kingdom in this sphere, one in which the God of heaven ruled and demonstrated His right to rule." [4] This is clearly seen in the garden where God gave Adam dominion over "every living thing."

There was one commandment given in the garden with consequence.

> *And the LORD God commanded the man, saying, Of every tree of the garden thou mayest freely eat: But of the tree of the knowledge of good and evil, thou shalt not eat of it: for in the day that thou eatest thereof thou shalt surely die. (Genesis 2:16-17)*

We don't know how long it was before Eve was visited by the serpent but we do know that one day the devil, disguised as a serpent, entered the garden. Speaking to Eve, the serpent said, "Yea, hath God said, Ye shall not eat of every tree of the garden?" (*Genesis 3:1*) Satan caused Eve to doubt God's word. Once we doubt the Word of God, we give the devil the foothold in our lives that he needs. Eve answered: "But of the fruit of the tree which is in the midst of the garden, God hath said, Ye shall not eat of it, neither shall ye touch it, lest ye die" *(Genesis 3:3)*.

Satan then lied to Eve by saying, "Ye shall not surely die." Then he mixed a lie with a bit of truth when he told her that if they ate from the tree their eyes would be opened and they would be like gods. Their eyes were opened to a knowledge they did not have before eating the fruit from this tree. The lie that they would be like gods was a temptation that was too great for Eve, and she took the fruit and ate from it. Apparently, Adam was right there with her though he never interfered or tried to stop the serpent from talking to Eve. Instead, he also ate of the fruit as Eve gave it to him. God had given the commandment to Adam, and he was the keeper of the garden and the leader of the family. He should have dealt with the serpent, not Eve. This great error led to the sinful downfall of not only Adam and Eve but of the whole human race that would come from them.

As Pentecost tells us, God had a purpose for testing Adam by prohibiting him to eat of the tree of knowledge of good and evil. Would the man recognize God's authority and subject himself to Him or would he think that he was not responsible or above God's law? "Those who are in the kingdom must obey the rule of the King. Obedience to that rule becomes a test as to whether one is in the kingdom." [5]

They were then cast out of the garden and out of God's presence, but the greater problem was that they now lost their position in the Kingdom of God and Satan now had dominion over them. Satan has since been known as the "ruler of this world" or the "prince of the power of the air."

When Adam and Eve heard the voice of God calling them in the garden in the cool of the day as He had done in times past, they hid themselves from Him and tied fig leaves around themselves to cover their nakedness. God called to them, "Where are you?" (*Genesis 3:9*). They answered, "We heard your voice in the garden and we were afraid because we are naked" (*Genesis 3:10*). God then answered, "Who told you that you were naked? Have you eaten of the tree I commanded you not to eat of?" (*Genesis 3:11*). Then Adam did what most of us sinners do when caught red-handed: he blamed someone else. In this case Adam said to God, "The woman whom thou gavest to be with me, she gave me of the tree, and I did eat" (*Genesis 3:12*). In other words, Adam blamed God for giving him the woman, and he blamed the woman for giving him the fruit. Never mind the fact that nobody told him to eat it.

God then turned to the woman, and she said, "The serpent beguiled me, and I did eat." In other words, she was saying that the devil made her do it! The word "beguiled" means "to lead astray." It is "a verb that means to deceive. It means to use deceptive methods or deceit to accomplish something: to deceive a person" [6]. This is exactly what the devil always does. He is a liar and a deceiver. The same tactics that the devil used to trick Eve into eating the fruit from the tree of the Knowledge of Good and Evil are the same ones that he uses to try to deceive us today. He appeals to the lust of our flesh, the lust of our eyes, and the pride of life (*1 John 2:16*). That's why the Apostle Paul tells us that "We are not ignorant of his devices" (*2 Corinthians 2:11*), we should not be ignorant of his evil schemes. For if we know God's Word, then we know how the evil one operates.

God then dealt with each one according to their sin. The serpent would now crawl on its belly all of its days and eat the dust of the earth. The woman would have pain in childbearing and her husband would have the rule over her. Adam would have to work the ground to make it bring forth fruit. Sin had entered the world and now death began both physically and spiritually in the bodies of Adam and Eve. This would be man's new nature, a sin nature, and this would be propagated to all of the human race, to all who come into this life through the seed of a man and woman. Now man would need redemption/salvation.

The Promise of a Redeemer

This prompted God to give Adam and Eve a promise. He would bring about a restoration for mankind in God's Kingdom. So, in the midst of a dark day, God gives hope to this first human family. He gave them the promise that one day, through the seed of a woman, God would send a Deliverer, A Redeemer, that would crush the head of the serpent (devil) and in the process, the heel of the deliverer would be bruised (*Genesis 3:15*). This is the first Messianic prophecy in the Bible given about 4,000 years before Jesus was born.

Though this prophecy was a long time in coming, one day Jesus was born in fulfillment of it. Jesus' death signaled the judgment of Satan. Adam and Eve were given the responsibility to rule this world, but because they sinned, they gave that rule to the devil. Now God had a plan to become a man to defeat the devil and be successful where Adam & Eve failed. Jesus' death meant the enemies defeat and through the cross of Christ, Jesus would deal with sin once, for all of humanity.

The Old Testament chronicles God desiring to set up His Kingdom on the earth through Israel, during the days of Jesus, but because Israel rejected Jesus Christ as their Messiah, He was unable to do so.

However, God did establish covenants with Israel, in the past, through great men of God who believed and obeyed His Word.

One such covenant was the Abrahamic Covenant, one that God made with Abraham. Through this covenant God promised that He would give the land of Canaan to Abraham's descendants forever. That land is what we know of today as the land of Israel. What God had formerly promised Abraham, He now confirmed by entering into the covenant with him.

In his book "Thy Kingdom Come", J. Dwight Pentecost explains two kinds of covenants into which God entered with Israel.

> *There were two kinds of covenants into which God entered with Israel: conditional and unconditional. In a conditional covenant, that which was covenanted depended on the recipient of the covenant for its fulfillment, not on the one making the covenant. Certain obligations or conditions would need to be kept by the recipient of the covenant before the giver of the covenant would be obligated to fulfill what was promised.* [7]

Pentecost gave the Mosaic Covenant as an example of a conditional covenant. Then he continues to tell of an unconditional covenant.

> *In an unconditional covenant, on the other hand, that which was covenanted depended for its fulfillment solely on the one making the covenant. That which was promised was sovereignly given to the recipient of the covenant on the authority and integrity of the one making the covenant, entirely apart from the merit or response of the receiver. It was a covenant with no "if" attached to it whatsoever.* [8]

God entered into an unconditional covenant with Abraham that his seed would possess the land of Canaan, and then in Genesis 17, God establishes this covenant to be an eternal or everlasting covenant. 2 Samuel 7 tells us that God also made an unconditional, eternal covenant with Israel's greatest king: King David. This covenant was known as the Davidic Covenant.

And when thy days be fulfilled, and thou shalt sleep with thy fathers, I will set up thy seed after thee, which shall proceed out of thy bowels, and I will establish his kingdom. He shall build an house for my name, and I will stablish the throne of his kingdom forever. I will be his father, and he shall be my son. If he commit iniquity, I will chasten him with the rod of men, and with the stripes of the children of men: But my mercy shall not depart away from him, as I took it from Saul, whom I put away before thee. And thine house and thy kingdom shall be established for ever before thee: thy throne shall be established forever. (2 Samuel 7:12-16)

This is also an unconditional covenant. Though there are no kings in Israel today and though Israel had been disobedient, Jesus came to fulfill the covenants He made with Abraham and David. The Abrahamic Covenant God made with Israel is an everlasting covenant, and it is because of this covenant that Jesus Christ will return at the Battle of Armageddon to fight for Israel. In the future, Jesus Christ will sit upon the throne of David, fulfilling the Davidic Covenant, ruling, and reigning in righteousness throughout the Millennial Reign of Jesus Christ. Our God is a promise keeper!

The Beginning of John's Ministry

Just before the coming of John the Baptist, there was a period of time known as the Four-Hundred Silent Years. They were "silent" because after the last prophet Malachi, who prophesied in approximately 396 BC, there were no other prophets or prophecies from heaven. The heavens were silent. John burst on the scene and began to preach repentance for the "Kingdom of Heaven is at hand" (Matthew 3:2). John had come to prepare the way for Jesus Christ as the scripture has said: "The voice of him that crieth in the wilderness, Prepare ye the way of the LORD, make straight in the desert a highway for our God" (Isaiah 40:3).

God's Kingdom through which comes God's right to rule had now immediately come upon the nation of Israel. Sadly though, Israel was not prepared for the good news that God's Kingdom would bring to them. John MacArthur expounds on this thought:

> *Now, when His word came to Israel again, proclaiming the coming of the King, it was not the expected word of joy and comfort and celebration but a message of warning and rebuke. The kingdom of heaven is at hand, waiting to be ushered in, but Israel was not ready for it. Despite many similar warnings by the prophets, many of the people and most leaders were not prepared for John's message.* [9]

As John's ministry was drawing to a close after the baptism of Jesus in the Jordan River, Jesus' ministry was just beginning.

The Kingdom of God through Jesus

The Bible points to Jesus coming not only to die for our sins but also to set up His Kingdom on earth. He said that His Kingdom was at hand, meaning *"to make near, approach, be at hand, come near, draw nigh"* [10]. Jesus was officially introducing Himself as the rightful heir to the throne of David according to the covenanted promise and was offering the kingdom to the covenanted people. While so many Christians believe that Jesus' primary teaching in the Gospels was on love, or peace, or faith, that is not the case. We must understand that in the Gospels, Jesus' main teaching was about the Kingdom of God. When Jesus came out of the wilderness being tempted of the devil, He proclaimed: "...The time is fulfilled, and the kingdom of God is at hand: repent ye, and believe the gospel" (*Mark 1:15*).

He taught about the Kingdom in Matthew Chapter 13 using the parables of the net, the mustard seed, the man who sowed good seed in his field, and the sower. He told us that before we were to seek Him for our needs, we should seek first the Kingdom of God and all His righteousness (*Matthew 6:33*).

Jesus was very clear in His teaching about entering His Kingdom. In one of Jesus' parables, He tells us about a certain householder which planted a vineyard and hedged it, dug a winepress in it and built a tower, and then let it out to husbandmen, and went into a far country. When the time of harvest drew near, the householder sent out his servants to gather the fruit. However, the husbandmen were deceitful, and they beat, stoned, and killed the man's servants. They even killed the householder's son. Jesus then asked them what they thought the lord of the vineyard would do to these husbandmen when he came to the vineyard?

> *They say unto him, He will miserably destroy those wicked men, and will let out his vineyard unto other husbandmen, which shall render him the fruits in their seasons. (Matthew 21:41)*

Jesus then answered them,

> *Therefore say I unto you, The kingdom of God shall be taken from you, and given to a nation bringing forth the fruits thereof. And when the chief priests and Pharisees had heard his parables, they perceived that he spake of them. (Matthew 21:43, 45)*

The Pharisees had misinterpreted the law through their traditions. Jesus called them out on this many times throughout the gospels, especially in the Sermon on the Mount in Matthew 5 through 7.

> *For I say unto you, That except your righteousness shall exceed the righteousness of the scribes and Pharisees, ye shall in no case enter into the kingdom of heaven. (Matthew 5:20)*

Jesus was prophesying that His Kingdom was near (*Matthew 4:17*). He sent His apostles out to preach that His Kingdom was at hand (*Matthew 10:7*). He went throughout Galilee preaching the gospel of the kingdom (*Matthew 4:23*). He told the unbelieving Pharisees, "But if I cast out devils by the Spirit of God, then the kingdom of God is come unto you" (*Matthew12:28*). Jesus gave Peter the Keys to the Kingdom of

Heaven (*Matthew* 16:19). He said it would be hard for a rich man to enter the kingdom (*Matthew* 19:23). Jesus said if we do not enter the kingdom as a little child, we cannot enter it (*Mark 10:15*).

Jesus always spoke of His Kingdom. Even when the Pharisees asked Him when the Kingdom of God should come, He told them that the kingdom doesn't come by observation, but that the kingdom is within you, meaning that His Kingdom is not a physical kingdom as the kingdoms of this world, but it is a spiritual kingdom. It's not a kingdom that can be seen but it is within you, within the heart. Jesus' major teaching was His Kingdom!

> *It is the peculiar business of Christ to establish the kingdom of heaven in the hearts of men. Yet he himself begins his preaching in the same words with John the Baptist, because the repentance which John taught, still was and ever will be the necessary preparation for that inward kingdom. But that phrase is not only used with regard to the individuals in whom this kingdom is to be established, but also with regard to the Christian church, —the whole body of believers.* [11]

Kingdom Matters: The Importance of Repentance

Repentance is also a major theme in the gospels and in the Book of Acts. John the Baptist was sent to prepare the way for Jesus' appearing. He did so by telling the people to repent because the Kingdom of God was coming to them. He baptized people unto repentance pointing the way to Jesus Christ.

> *I indeed baptize you with water unto repentance: but he that cometh after me is mightier than I, whose shoes I am not worthy to bear: he shall baptize you with the Holy Ghost, and with fire. (Matthew 3:11)*

What is Repentance? Although repentance involves having sorrow for the sins we have committed, the meaning goes far deeper. Repentance is a turning away from our sinful life, and it is a turning to God. It does involve confession of our sins before God *(1 John 1:9)*. Repentance involves a change of our hearts, minds, actions, and our wills. David Bernard says this of repentance:

> *It is a voluntary act of man in response to the call of God. It denotes an active turn, not just a feeling of regret or an apology. It is more than a moral resolution or reformation; it is a spiritual decision and a spiritual change.* [12]

It is doing a complete 180-degree about-face. When John the Baptist came preaching repentance, he told the people to "Bring forth therefore fruits meet for repentance" *(Matthew 3:8)*. The New Living Translation of the Bible helps us to understand this verse a little better: "Prove by the way you live that you have repented of your sins and turned to God" *(Matthew 3:8-9 NLT)*.

When true repentance has happened the individual will show forth works that are consistent with a repentant life. A good example of repentance would be the Apostle Paul. After his conversion he was as zealous for the kingdom of God as he was against it before he met Jesus on the road to Damascus. Paul made a complete turnaround. Repentance was necessary for the preparation for the coming of the Messiah as foretold in the prophecies. The human heart is a wicked thing. Jeremiah the prophet said of the heart: "The heart is deceitful above all things, and desperately wicked: who can know it?" The Apostle Paul wrote:

> *For I know that in me (that is, in my flesh,) dwelleth no good thing: for to will is present with me; but how to perform that which is good I find not. (Romans 7:18)*

Only as we pour our hearts out through repentance can our hearts be truly cleansed of all the filthiness of the flesh and the spirit and be in right standing with God.

Kingdom Matters: You Must Be Born Again!

How are we to enter into the Kingdom of God? Does the Bible show us the way that we are to enter into the Kingdom of Heaven? The third chapter of the Gospel of John is a story about Jesus and a man named Nicodemus. Nicodemus was a Pharisee, and it seems like he may have believed the possibility that Jesus might be the Messiah. He said to Jesus, "we know that you have come from God because no one can do the miracles that you have been doing, except you are from above" *(John 3:2)*. Jesus' reply to Nicodemus was this: "...Verily, verily, I say unto thee, Except a man be born again, he cannot see the kingdom of God" *(John 3:3)*.

Why did Jesus say that we must be born again? As sinful human beings, God's kingdom is unattainable to us through any natural means. Since through our first birth we are unable to enter into God's Kingdom, due to sin, God made a way through the expiatory sacrifice of Jesus Christ for us to be born again into His Kingdom. This is what Peter, Paul, and the rest of the apostles preached after Jesus returned to heaven. It is the gospel defined by Paul in 1 Corinthians:

> *Moreover, brethren, I declare unto you the gospel which I preached unto you, which also ye have received, and wherein ye stand; By which also ye are saved, if ye keep in memory what I preached unto you, unless ye have believed in vain. For I delivered unto you first of all that which I also received, how that Christ died for our sins according to the scriptures; And that he was buried, and that he rose again the third day according to the scriptures: (1 Corinthians 15:1-4)*

Now Nicodemus questioned what Jesus had just said. He asked, "How can I be born again? It is impossible for me to re-enter my mother's womb." Of course, Nicodemus was just thinking in the natural. Jesus' answer was regarding a spiritual birth which laid the foundation that Jesus was speaking of a heavenly and not an earthly kingdom.

Jesus was emphatic about this: "Ye Must Be Born Again" if you want to see the Kingdom of God. How to enter this heavenly Kingdom is what the rest of this book is all about. Scripture lays this out for us to see in the Book of the Acts of the Apostles. (*This could only have been possible after Jesus had ascended back into heaven.*) So, Jesus gave him a little more information when He said: "...Verily, verily, I say unto thee, Except a man be born of water and of the Spirit, he cannot enter into the kingdom of God" (*John 3:5*).

As one would enter this world through a birth of water and spirit, so must we enter God's Kingdom by being born into it, a birth of water and Spirit. That this was Jesus' meaning is expressed in the next two verses which say: "That which is born of the flesh is flesh; and that which is born of the Spirit is spirit. Marvel not that I said unto thee, Ye must be born again" (*John 3:6-7*).

Our original earthly birth of water is when we are encased in our mother's womb, totally submerged in amniotic fluid. Having no or little amniotic fluid is a very serious condition which could put the baby at risk. Modern medicine today can at times provide necessary treatment to save the baby but in Bible days this may not have been possible. If there was no water birth the baby could die. If the baby was born of the water but the baby's lungs did not respond after birth, then the baby would be a stillborn, no birth of spirit. Using the same comparison, our spiritual birth must be one of water and Spirit. In John 3:8, it says:

> *The wind bloweth where it listeth, and thou hearest the sound thereof, but canst not tell whence it cometh, and whither it goeth: so is everyone that is born of the Spirit.*

Why is being born again compared to the wind blowing? The following is a paraphrase of verse 8 from the book, *John, the Gospel That Had to be Written*:

> *The birth of the Spirit is like the wind blowing. The wind blows where it wants to, and you have no control over it. But you know when it's blowing*

because you hear its sound. It has its own language. So is everyone who is born of the Spirit. You can't control the Spirit, but you know when you are born of the Spirit for you will hear the voice of the Spirit speaking when entering your being! [13]

In general, Jesus seems to be saying, "Nicodemus, you have been born into this world as a sinful human being. Now you must be born again by a spiritual new birth, especially if you want to see the Kingdom of God. As the Apostle Paul wrote in 1 Corinthians 15:50, "... Flesh and blood cannot inherit the kingdom of God, neither doth corruption inherit incorruption." Therefore, we must undergo a complete spiritual transformation, and God accomplishes this in us through the New Birth.

Final Thoughts

God, our Creator, is also a very personal God. He desires for each one of us to live with Him in Heaven throughout eternity. However, to be truly honest, not one of us, by our own merit, is worthy of heaven because we are sinful creatures. But because of the love and mercy of Almighty God, He made it possible for His Kingdom to become attainable. It is by His grace for all those who will seek Him. Jesus died on Calvary so that our sins would be forgiven and now, regardless of our past life, Jesus offers us eternal life. We receive this *new life* when we are born again of water and Spirit.

As the Word says, "for whosoever will..." Your future is bright when you pursue God and His Kingdom.

2

YE SHALL RECEIVE POWER

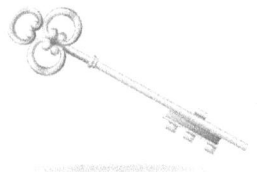

In 2006 my wife and I were living in South Carolina and attending a Spanish Church under the leadership of Reverend Victor M. Melendez. He was a very humble and compassionate man, but also a powerful man of God. One Wednesday evening while we were having a mid-week Bible study, a young couple entered the room. They looked quite ordinary, and everything was going well until Bro. Melendez finished speaking and invited the people to come to the altar to pray. He went down to meet the new couple and as he walked toward them the woman locked eyes on his and then she started to scream and became combative with him. Bro. Melendez later told me that as he approached them, he knew that the woman was demon-possessed because while pastoring in Brooklyn, New York, he had many such encounters.

We had to subdue her and wrestle her to the ground. She was a very thin young lady, but she seemed to have a lot of strength. Her face had a contorted, angry look with blood shot eyes, and she was screaming. As we had prayed over her, many demons were cast out through the power of God. After a while when she had calmed down Pastor

Melendez asked her if she wanted to be baptized in the Name of Jesus Christ. She said she did.

She was then given a baptismal robe and she came up the steps towards the baptismal tank when all of a sudden, she started to slither away. Bro. Melendez picked up on what she was doing, and he caught her by the ankle and drew her into the baptismal tank. Apparently, there was still a demon hiding within her. As soon as she went into the water, she coughed up some hideous looking phlegm, something like I've never seen before. He put her under the water in Jesus' Name and she came out raising her hands in praise to God; her bloodshot eyes were now clear, her face no longer contorted. The demon within her was so fearful of the Name of Jesus that he fled from her before we even baptized her. It was then that I received the amazing revelation of the power of the Name of Jesus. We didn't have to cast him out of her; he left, in fear, of his own accord.

Miracles, signs, and wonders are often talked about as a mystery, and often dismissed as a fluke. But that is not the case at all, as we will see in chapter 3. The same power that Jesus displayed when He lived among us, is for us and is available to us through His Spirit.

Let's start by examining the Book of Acts

The Book of Acts is the continuing work of Jesus Christ through His Apostles. He did not leave them as orphans, but He promised that He would be with them even unto the end of the age and that He would empower them with His Spirit. He vowed that He would send the promise of the Father, which is the Holy Ghost. Although Jesus would not be with them physically any longer, He would now live within them spiritually, and they would be empowered by His Spirit.

The book of Acts recounts the acts or actions of the Apostles after Christ's ascension, as a new day was dawning for the world. The Church Jesus established would be born in power and in a blaze of glory on the first Pentecost Sunday as explained in the second chapter of Acts. This book is the history of the Church as the Apostles carried out the express commands of Jesus Christ as He gave them in the Great Commission (*Matthew 27:19-20; Mark 16:15-18; Luke 24:46-49; John 20:21-23*). Jesus would give them the power through His Holy Spirit so that they could continue the ministry of the Spirit to heal the sick, cast out devils, and do whatever was needed to accomplish the will of God. Jesus said in John 14:12 that we would do greater works than He did. Most commentators believe that the "works" in this scripture refers mainly to greater quantity. Through the Holy Spirit in His believers, Jesus will touch more people than He was able to touch while on earth, through the preaching of the Word, with miraculous signs following. As Tony Merida stated in *Christ-Centered Exposition*: "Acts is not merely the history of the early church; it is the history of the mission of the early church." [1]

The Gospel of Luke

Luke was a physician who is credited with writing the Gospel of Luke. He then wrote the Acts of the Apostles as a sequel to his Gospel account of Jesus. He was the only Gentile known to write a book in the New Testament. He was a close companion and friend with the Apostle Paul. [2]

Luke recounts how *many* people have written about the things that have been believed among the early Christians.

> *Forasmuch as many have taken in hand to set forth in order a declaration of those things which are most surely believed among us, Even as they delivered them unto us, which from the beginning were eyewitnesses, and ministers of the word; It seemed good to me also, having had perfect understanding of all things from the very first, to write unto thee in order, most excellent Theophilus, That thou mightest know the certainty of those things, wherein thou hast been instructed. (Luke 1:1-4)*

These things written about Jesus were handed down to the believers from "eyewitnesses," those who had seen firsthand the things which Jesus did and taught during His years of ministry on earth. So then, Luke is not writing his Gospel as a firsthand account, as he was not an eyewitness, but as one who also had to receive it from others. Most scholars believe that Luke received much of his knowledge about Jesus from the Apostle Paul as he traveled with him at times as evidenced in the Book of Acts. "It is also widely agreed that Luke consulted with 'other apostles' in addition to Paul in the writing of his gospel, as he testifies in his prologue." [3]

Who were the *many*? These would have had to be the Twelve Apostles who lived and walked with Jesus. They saw Him die and they saw Him after His death. Scripture tells us that after His resurrection they even examined the wounds in His hands and His side as a confirmation that it was truly Him (*John 20:20,27; Luke 24:39*). Another eyewitness may have been Mark the writer of the Gospel that bears his name, although Mark was not an eyewitness himself, but it is believed that he wrote his Gospel through the eyes of Peter. Mary, the mother of Jesus could have narrated the stories of Gabriel's annunciation to her and Zechariah to Luke (*Luke 1:26-37*). Only Zechariah could have known exactly what happened in the temple when Gabriel appeared to him (*Luke 1:5-25*). Mary Magdalene and some of the other women could have told the story of what happened at the tomb on Resurrection morning, as they were the first to see the empty tomb (*Mark 16:1-8*).

> *It was Mary Magdalene, and Joanna, and Mary the mother of James, and other women that were with them, which told these things unto the apostles. (Luke 24:10)*

There were many others, such as the seventy who Jesus sent out to preach the Gospel (*Luke 10:1-12*), many of the women who ministered to Him, the 120 in the upper room, and those 500 who Paul mentions in 1 Corinthians 15:6. Here are some Scriptural confirmations:

> *After that, he was seen of above five hundred brethren at once; of whom the greater part remain unto this present, but some are fallen asleep. (1 Corinthians 15:6)*

Luke, being an accurate historian, had carefully investigated all that had been handed down to him, and having had knowledge of all these things from the beginning, had set out to write an orderly account to a Most Excellent Theophilus. What had been handed down to him gave Luke the research he needed to write this orderly account of the Life of Jesus Christ. *The New American Commentary* explained this term "orderly:"

> *The term orderly was used throughout Greek literature by writers who sought to convince their hearers of the meticulous research and careful organization of their material. By his use of this term Luke was stating that he had written his Gospel in a logical fashion. In the next verse he gives the purpose of this meticulous research and orderly writing.* [4]

Luke 1, verses 3 and 4, tells us that Luke was writing this Gospel to a particular person: one named Theophilus. We know little of Theophilus: who he was, where he was from, or how he was related to Luke. The fact that Luke addressed him as "most excellent" shows that he was probably of an upper class or level of society. Who was Theophilus? What do we know of him?

> *Theophilus (theos = God + philos = friend) means "friend of God" or "God lover." In the beginning of his Gospel, Luke addresses Theophilus as most excellent Theophilus (Luke 1:3), which was a way to address someone who held a high office. It is a title of honor and rank. Most commentators agree that Theophilus was almost certainly a real person, probably a patron or sponsor of Luke.* [5]

From these examples, Luke's purpose in writing was to give Theophilus a true and accurate account of the life and ministry of Jesus

Christ so that he could be safe and secure in the knowledge of the Lord. From this passage, and from the first four verses of Acts Chapter 1, it is possible that Theophilus was either a Christian or he may have been seriously considering becoming one.

> *As a historian, Luke claims that he was not only accurate in his investigation into these things...but he traced these events and accounts back to their origins. The purpose of this study was to present an account...of Jesus' life that was clear, logical, and easily understood...Thus Luke's narrative served to affirm the accuracy and validity...of the teaching Theophilus was receiving regarding the Christian faith.* [6]

Acts: Luke's Second Book

Interestingly, the Book of Acts is a continuation of Luke's gospel. As John Stott explained:

> *It [the Gospel of Luke] was first (protos) which can refer to the first in a set, in this case first Luke's Gospel, then his book of Acts which picks up where the Gospel ended, with Jesus' crucifixion, burial and resurrection. It is interesting that at one time the Gospel of Luke and the Book of Acts were joined together as one book composed of two volumes.* [7]

This continuation can be seen by reading the first words of the Book of Acts:

> *The former treatise have I made, O Theophilus, of all that Jesus began both to do and teach, Until the day in which he was taken up, after that he through the Holy Ghost had given commandments unto the apostles whom he had chosen: (Acts 1:1-2)*

As the Book of Acts opens, Jesus is about to ascend up into heaven, and before He does, He tells His Apostles not to depart from Jerusalem but to wait for the Promise of the Father, which is the promise of the

Holy Ghost. Jesus then ascended into heaven after He had lived, was crucified, died, was buried, and rose from the dead. This departure of Jesus must have been a very painful thing for those who were so close to Him during His 3 ½ years of ministry on the earth.

Now the Apostles would be charged with the mission to continue the work that Jesus had started. They were to proclaim the Gospel of the Kingdom of God everywhere they went, and they were to do this without the physical presence of Jesus that had previously enabled their efforts. They wouldn't be able to stand with Him anymore as He healed the sick, raised the dead, and forgave the sinner. No longer could they hope to see the marvel of His power as He calmed the storm at sea and cast out devils by His word alone. Now everything Jesus had started was left to these 12 ordinary men to continue so that Jesus' sacrifice would not be in vain. In Albert Barnes Commentary on Acts 1:1, it says:

> *Since these events pertained to the descent of the Spirit, to the spread of the gospel, to the organization of the church, to the kind of preaching by which the church was to be collected and organized, and as the facts in the case constituted a full proof of the truth of the Christian religion, and the conduct of the apostles <u>would be a model for ministers and the church in all future times</u>, it was of great importance that a fair and full narrative of these things should be preserved.* [8]

Mr. Barnes is correct in his assertions, especially when he says that *"the facts in the case constituted a full proof of the truth of the Christian religion,"* and the conduct of the apostles *"would be a model for ministers and the church in all future times."* I surmise it is for that reason that Luke wanted to give Theophilus an authentic narrative because of the possibility that there would arise many exaggerated accounts. If we want to be apostolic in our belief, we need to follow this model found in the Book of the Acts of the Apostles instead of following the path of the reformers.

Divine Instructions to Change the World

In the first 3 verses of Acts 1, Luke explains to Theophilus that he is writing about what "Jesus began both to do and teach." Luke relates that Jesus gave the Apostles special instructions and then was taken up into heaven. These instructions are discovered in the Great Commission, which is found at the end of each Gospel account. Jesus is telling the Apostles to take His Gospel and preach it to the whole world. The Book of Acts continues by revealing how the Church was born and how the Apostles carried out that Great Commission through the power of the Holy Spirit. The Life Application Commentary on Acts explains this more fully:

> *Luke set out to explain the entire gospel story to Theophilus, telling him about everything Jesus began to do and teach until the day he was taken up to heaven after giving his chosen apostles further instructions through the Holy Spirit. The translation 'began to do and teach' shows that the books of Luke and Acts give the accurate account of the beginning of all that Christ was to do on earth. The book of Acts would show the continuation of his work on earth through his church, his body.* [9]

It continues by saying:

> *Before he 'ascended to heaven' the resurrected Christ taught his disciples for forty days. In that short period, he gave those 'chosen apostles' the instruction that would radically change their lives and, through them, the world. The fact that the apostles have been chosen by Christ (Luke 6:12-16) is an extremely important point. With that choosing came apostolic authority to preach, teach, direct the church, and preserve the record of his life and teaching...* [10]

> *Luke records only a handful of sentences from those forty days of instruction, so they certainly are important words. These statements of Jesus are*

loaded with significance, giving us not only the outline of the book of Acts, but the general outline of church history. [11]

Let's understand what is being said here. The Apostles were given exact instructions that would "radically change not only their lives, but the whole world." Therefore, what we shall see as we continue through the book is that what is recorded in the Book of Acts is precisely what Jesus told the Apostles to do once they received the power of the Holy Ghost. We will see how the Apostles responded to men when, after the preaching and teaching of the Word, they were convicted of their sins and wanted to know how to be saved. How did the Apostles and Paul respond? We will revisit this theme later on in the book. It makes one wonder; how did we drift so far away from what was first preached by the Apostles on that first Pentecost Sunday?

Luke's Purpose: Jesus Is Alive!

> *To whom also he shewed himself alive after his passion by many infallible proofs, being seen of them forty days, and speaking of the things pertaining to the kingdom of God... (Acts 1:3)*

One clear purpose for Luke writing his gospel and Acts was to plainly show the evidence of Christ's resurrection and promise of return. The Apostles were convinced that Jesus was alive after they saw the nail prints in His hands and feet and saw the hole in His side where He was pierced by the Roman sword. Jesus even asked them to touch Him in order to prove that He had a resurrected body, a body with flesh and bone and was not a ghost or spirit.

> *And he said unto them, Why are ye troubled? and why do thoughts arise in your hearts? Behold my hands and my feet, that it is I myself: handle me, and see; for a spirit hath not flesh and bones, as ye see me have. (Luke 24:38-39)*

The Apostles ate fish with Him on the seashore and they saw Him come and go from their presence, just disappearing out of their sight. Later these things caused Peter to write to those who would be around after his death:

> *Moreover I will endeavor that ye may be able after my decease to have these things always in remembrance. For we have not followed cunningly devised fables, when we made known unto you the power and coming of our Lord Jesus Christ but were eyewitnesses of his majesty. (2 Peter 1:15-16)*

These Apostles were so convinced that Jesus was truly alive, even though many Jews opposed them and even spread a rumor that the Apostles came and stole away the body of Jesus Christ (*Matthew 28:12-15*). They were so convinced that they all died a martyr's death, except John. Now, who would be willing to die for a hoax, or for something that they knew was not true? No, Jesus had risen, just as He said He would, and now they were first hand eyewitnesses of all that Jesus taught and did. He is seated at the right hand of God. Not only that, He made a clear path for us to enter His kingdom and rule with Him.

Connecting the Scripture: The Promise of the Father

It seems that according to verses 4-5 of Acts Chapter 1, Jesus' final command to His disciples was to wait for the Promise of the Father (*John 15:26, 16:7-8*). He said:

> *And, being assembled together with them, commanded them that they should not depart from Jerusalem, but wait for the promise of the Father, which, saith he, ye have heard of me. For John truly baptized with water; but ye shall be baptized with the Holy Ghost not many days hence. (Acts 1:4-5)*

This promise of the Father is a four-thousand-year-old promise originally given to Adam and Eve. Through this promise, God is letting the whole world know that someday in the future a man child, the seed of a woman, would be born that would change the entire world. This is the first Messianic prophecy in the Bible.

> *And I will put enmity between thee and the woman, and between thy seed and her seed; it shall bruise thy head, and thou shalt bruise his heel. (Genesis 3:15)*

About two thousand years later, God called Abram out of Ur of the Chaldees. God made some promises to Abram that would concern his physical descendants, his future generations, forever. It was a promise that would be passed down through Isaac, then Jacob, and then to the twelve tribes of Israel. The Old Testament scriptures sometimes refer to a man's descendants as a "seed." Notice how God affirms His promise to Abram:

> *And the LORD appeared unto Abram, and said, Unto thy seed will I give this land: and there builded he an altar unto the LORD, who appeared unto him. (Genesis 12:7)*

> *And I will make thy seed as the dust of the earth: so that if a man can number the dust of the earth, then shall thy seed also be numbered. (Genesis 13:16)*

But God also promised Abram that "in thee shall all families of the earth be blessed" (*Genesis 12:3*). This promise would be fulfilled through a physical descendant of Abraham, Jesus Christ, some 2000 years later. The Apostle Paul said in Galatians:

> *Now to Abraham and his seed were the promises made. He saith not, And to seeds, as of many; but as of one, And to thy seed, which is Christ. (Galatians 3:16)*

Paul is making an argument here to the Judaizers (*Jews or Jewish Christians*) that the covenant of promise made to Abraham 430 years before the law was given to Moses cannot be disannulled by the law. He said in Galatians 3:16 that the promise was made to Abraham and his seed, not to seeds as being many, but to one seed which was Christ. This was the promise of the Father that Jesus spoke of in John:

> *And I will pray the Father, and he shall give you another Comforter, that he may abide with you for ever; Even the Spirit of truth; whom the world cannot receive, because it seeth him not, neither knoweth him: but ye know him; for he dwelleth with you, and shall be in you. (John 14:16-17)*

And the same promise Peter spoke of on the Day of Pentecost:

> *Therefore being by the right hand of God exalted, and having received of the Father the promise of the Holy Ghost, he hath shed forth this, which ye now see and hear. (Acts 2:33)*

The promise of God to Adam and Eve was the promise of a "seed," and the promise made to Abraham was also a promise of a "seed." The "seed" in both the promises is speaking of one and the same person, Jesus Christ, the Savior of the world. And it is through this promise that all the nations of the world would be blessed. This promise would be fulfilled when the Gentiles received the gift of the Holy Ghost in Acts Chapter 10. Many of the prophets foretold of this promise of the outpouring of the Holy Ghost:

> *For I will pour water upon him that is thirsty, and floods upon the dry ground: I will pour my spirit upon thy seed, and my blessing upon thine offspring: (Isaiah 44:3)*

> *Whom shall he teach knowledge? and whom shall he make to understand doctrine? them that are weaned from the milk, and drawn from the breasts.*

For precept must be upon precept, precept upon precept; line upon line, line upon line; here a little, and there a little: For with stammering lips and another tongue will he speak to this people. To whom he said, This is the rest wherewith ye may cause the weary to rest; and this is the refreshing: yet they would not hear. But the word of the LORD was unto them precept upon precept, precept upon precept; line upon line, line upon line; here a little, and there a little; that they might go, and fall backward, and be broken, and snared, and taken. (Isaiah 28:9-13)

A new heart also will I give you, and a new spirit will I put within you: and I will take away the stony heart out of your flesh, and I will give you an heart of flesh. And I will put my spirit within you, and cause you to walk in my statutes, and ye shall keep my judgments, and do them. (Ezekiel 36:26-27)

And it shall come to pass afterward, that I will pour out my spirit upon all flesh; and your sons and your daughters shall prophesy, your old men shall dream dreams, your young men shall see visions: And also upon the servants and upon the handmaids in those days will I pour out my spirit. (Joel 2:27-29)

Jesus also told His apostles of this promise:

But when the Comforter is come, whom I will send unto you from the Father, even the Spirit of truth, which proceedeth from the Father, he shall testify of me... (John 15:26)

And when John the Baptist saw the Pharisees and Sadducees come to his baptism he said:

I indeed baptize you with water unto repentance: but he that cometh after me is mightier than I, whose shoes I am not worthy to bear: he shall baptize you with the Holy Ghost, and with fire: (Matthew 3:11)

This promise of the Father is what the 120 believers in the upper room received on that first Pentecost Sunday morning as they all spoke in tongues as the Holy Spirit gave them utterance.

A Question Concerning the Kingdom

While they were assembled together, the Apostles asked Jesus a question concerning the Kingdom of God:

When they therefore were come together, they asked of him, saying, Lord, wilt thou at this time restore again the kingdom to Israel? And he said unto them, It is not for you to know the times or the seasons, which the Father hath put in his own power. (Acts 1:6-7)

This brings up an important question because it is apparent that Jesus did not restore the Kingdom at this time. Also, what the Jews were expecting their Messiah to do when He came was totally different from what Jesus' mission was at His first coming. They were expecting the Messiah to restore Israel as a nation again by defeating and destroying the Roman Empire. However, when Jesus came this first time, He came as a baby in a manger; he came to die on a cross for our sins. The Jewish leaders could not accept Jesus because of this, and they rejected Him. Jesus therefore postponed setting up His Kingdom on earth for about 2,000 years. That is why Jesus was seen lamenting over Israel in these verses of scripture:

O Jerusalem, Jerusalem, thou that killest the prophets, and stonest them which are sent unto thee, how often would I have gathered thy children together, even as a hen gathereth her chickens under her wings, and ye would not! Behold, your house is left unto you desolate. (Matthew 23:37-38)

And when he was come near, he beheld the city, and wept over it, Saying, If thou hadst known, even thou, at least in this thy day, the things which belong unto thy peace! But now they are hid from thine eyes. For the days shall come upon thee, that thine enemies shall cast a trench about thee, and compass thee round, and keep thee in on every side, And shall lay thee even with the ground, and thy children within thee; and they shall leave in thee one stone upon another; because thou knewest not the time of thy visitation. (Luke 19:41-44)

Jesus came proclaiming that the Kingdom of Heaven was at hand, meaning that the Kingdom of God was coming near, approaching, or drawing nigh (*Matthew 4:17*). However, since they rejected Him, He warned them that troublesome times would come upon them and that the great temple in Jerusalem would be thrown down, and that one stone would not be seen laying upon another. This was fulfilled in 70 A.D when the Romans, led by General Titus, came and destroyed the city of Jerusalem. Over one million Jews lost their lives during the siege.

Tony Evans wrote that while it was not yet the time for Christ's millennial kingdom to arrive but it was the time for the Holy Spirit to come. "The disciples were not permitted to know the timing of the establishment of the kingdom, but they would not need to wait much longer to experience the power of the kingdom." [12] These same twelve men who before Pentecost fled and left Jesus during his arrest for fear; this same Peter who denied His Lord three times would now would boldly stand against the Jewish leaders and proclaim that they had crucified the Lord and called them to repent of their sins and turn to God. These same Apostles would perform miracles, preach the Word without fear or favor, the power of God coursing through them.

The Kingdom's Mission: The Church

The Kingdom's mission from the Book of Acts to today is simple but not always easy. Jesus left His apostles with a mission: we are to go spread the hope of Christ and to share His glorious Gospel. In order to accomplish this great mission, Jesus gave the apostles a great promise:

> *But ye shall receive power, after that the Holy Ghost is come upon you: and ye shall be witnesses unto me both in Jerusalem, and in all Judaea, and in Samaria, and unto the uttermost part of the earth. (Acts 1:8)*

This statement made by Jesus is the mission of the Church! The disciples received the power to become witnesses for Jesus after they were filled with the Holy Ghost. And it is after we receive the Holy Ghost that we are endued with power to become witnesses for Jesus so that we can bring His saving message to all the world. It is only by this power of Christ in us that we can be bold witnesses, truly fulfilling God's purpose for us. We will need this power if we are to endure persecution, as they did in the early church. As Tony Merida says in Exalting Jesus in Acts:

> *Even this is part of God's ordained means of advancing the gospel – dedicated believers share his truth wherever they go, in spite of what they encounter. The gospel never triumphs apart from some measure of sacrifice. Someone has to sacrifice (and sometimes die) so that others may live.* [13]

These strong words are not for the faint of heart. Many of these early Christians died for their faith in Christ. It is very possible as we approach closer to the time of Jesus' 2nd coming, that we may see and experience persecution, where our very lives may be in danger. We must have our minds made-up now, what we will do in those times. That will not be a time where we will have the ability to call our Pastor to ask him what we should do. That will not be a time where we can wait on God for an answer. We must have a made-up mind and a fixed heart and be ready to die for the Lord, if that is His will!

After Jesus said these things in Acts 1:8, He ascended into the heavens and a cloud received Him out of their sight. They were all in awe as they just stood around looking, watching, as Jesus ascended into heaven. There were two men (these were angels) that were standing by in white apparel, and they said,

Ye men of Galilee, why stand ye gazing up into heaven? This same Jesus, which is taken up from you into heaven, shall so come in like manner as ye have seen him go into heaven. (Acts 1:11)

Today we are at the point in history when this prophecy by the angels is about to be fulfilled upon the earth. Jesus is coming back, and He is coming soon! When He comes, He will be touching down right where the angels said He would, on the Mount of Olives in Jerusalem. Jesus is coming this time not as a baby in a manger; He is not coming riding on a donkey, but on a horse. He is not coming to die but He is coming in all His power and glory as King of Kings and Lord of Lords and He will defend Israel against the nations of the world. This time is more appropriately known as the "Day of the Lord" and the great battle that He will fight is known as the Battle of Armageddon. After these things take place, Jesus Christ will then set up His Kingdom and He will reign in righteousness and peace.

Final Thoughts

Brothers and Sisters, friends, neighbors, do you know that we are living in a time that theologians call the End of the Age? John was a voice crying out in the wilderness to warn the Israelites that their Messiah was coming soon. Even so, I and many others are warning this generation that we are on the precipice of the Second Coming of the Lord Jesus Christ!

I am writing about the infallible Word of God and the Kingdom of God which is within us and is advancing through the power of His Spirit! It's about the trustworthy prophecies in the Bible that have never failed and will never fail. Just look around you and what do you see? War and unrest in almost every part of the globe. Sin and sinners are getting worse and worse. In fact, that is a biblical example of what will happen in the end times.

> *But evil men and seducers shall wax worse and worse, deceiving, and being deceived. (2 Timothy 3:13)*

> *This know also, that in the last days perilous times shall come. (2 Timothy 3:1)*

During this time many people who do not know the Lord will be living in fear. Jesus said,

> *Men's hearts failing them for fear, and for looking after those things which are coming on the earth: for the powers of heaven shall be shaken. (Luke 21:26)*

Both the writings of Paul to Timothy and Luke to Theophilus are speaking of the same time period, and it seems that it is remarkably close to the time that we are living in. There will be many people that will be living in fear because of the things that will be happening on earth. And that is why we need to be aware of what is coming upon our world in the near future. As the scripture says:

> *And such as do wickedly against the covenant shall he corrupt by flatteries: but the people that do know their God shall be strong and do exploits. And they that understand among the people shall instruct many: (Daniel 11:32)*

Today we are living out the last days of the Book of the Acts of the Apostles. Although we are not eyewitnesses as the disciples of Jesus were then, we have the firsthand account of the words and works of the Apostles as given to them by Jesus Christ through His Word recorded by Luke in the Book of Acts. This ministry the Lord Jesus began in Acts Chapter 2 is still alive and continuing today. We may be the Lord's Church of the last days, and we shall have the power to be strong and do exploits. We may be called upon by many to instruct them on what to do as this evil world begins to encroach upon them.

Will we be ready? Will we answer the call? Are we going to faithfully share in God's work in these last days?

3
WHAT MEANETH THIS?

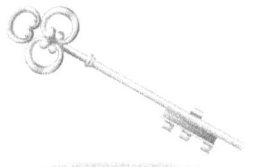

Have you ever anticipated receiving a gift? I can remember when I was a young boy that I wanted this certain gift for Christmas. It was called "The Astro Base," and it was a big rocket ship that had a door on the side of it. An astronaut figure came out on a crane. The crane would then lower him and release him into a motorized car that was remotely controlled. It was a very cool gift. I remember asking my parents to get it for me. Knowing it was quite an expensive gift, it was the only gift I asked for that year. When Christmas came that year and I was handed this big box, I knew I had received what I asked for. It was a great gift, and it made me happy.

The Gift of the Holy Ghost was a gift that had been prophesied about for many centuries. However, on a particular day, Pentecost Sunday, which was an important Jewish Feast Day, God gave humanity the greatest gift we could ever receive. On that day, God put a part of Himself into unworthy "earthen vessels." The wonderful thing is that it was not only given to the first Century Church, but it is given to anyone who will believe and obey the Gospel of Jesus Christ. Even in this 21st Century, people are receiving the Gift of the Holy Ghost just like the Apostles did on that first Pentecost Sunday.

And when the day of Pentecost was fully come, they were all with one accord in one place. And suddenly there came a sound from heaven as of a rushing mighty wind, and it filled all the house where they were sitting. And there appeared unto them cloven tongues like as of fire, and it sat upon each of them. And they were all filled with the Holy Ghost, and began to speak with other tongues, as the Spirit gave them utterance. (Acts 2:1-4)

What is Pentecost?

Pentecost is the second of the three great spring festivals of Israel. It indicated the time of the wheat harvest and it celebrated the day Moses received the Law on Mt. Sinai. The word Pentecost means "fiftieth" because it was celebrated 50 days after the Feast of the Passover. It was also called the Feast of Weeks [1]. R.C. Sproul speaks of the Feast of Pentecost in his Commentary:

It was the Jewish Thanksgiving of the Old Testament. It was also called the Feast of Firstfruits because, since the arid climate of Palestine has two rainy seasons , they had two growing seasons, a former season and a latter season. They would celebrate at the former rains and again at the latter rains. People gathered for the Thanksgiving event of Pentecost at the central sanctuary in Jerusalem to thank God for the harvest. [2]

When the Day of Pentecost had fully come, that is, when it had fully arrived, the Old Testament prophecies were about to be fulfilled. According to God's perfect timing, on the morning of the Jewish Feast of Pentecost, the 120 had gathered together. They were all in "one accord and in one place," as the scripture says, and God began to pour out His Holy Spirit on all those present. Those who had been filled with the Holy Ghost were acting quite lively and peculiar. The noise brought a crowd from Jerusalem to see what was going on. When they arrived, they all heard the 120 speaking in their own native language (*there were approximately 15-17 different languages represented by the crowd*), a language that those unlearned Galileans had never been taught. Some were amazed and some doubted, but it could not be denied that some incredible thing happened that day in Jerusalem.

The Importance of Unity

What does it mean to be in "one accord"? According to the "Complete Word Study Dictionary, New Testament," the phrase "in one accord" is the Greek word "homothumos" which means to be of one mind, unanimous consent, in one accord, all together. [3] There is something to be said about a group of people being together in unity. Their minds and hearts were concentrated on receiving the Promise of the Father. For ten days they had been waiting, most likely praying, and even fasting during this time. Maybe they were discussing exactly how Jesus was going to send this promise to them. Paul speaks of the importance of unity in the church in 1 Corinthians:

> *Now I beseech you, brethren, by the name of our Lord Jesus Christ, that ye all speak the same thing, and that there be no divisions among you; but that ye be perfectly joined together in the same mind and in the same judgment. (1 Corinthians 1:10)*

> *But I urge and entreat you, brethren, by the name of our Lord Jesus Christ, that all of you be in perfect harmony and full agreement in what you say, and that there be no dissensions or factions or divisions among you, but that you be perfectly united in your common understanding and in your opinions and judgments.*
> *(1 Corinthians 1:10 AMP)*

Unity doesn't mean that we do everything the same and always agree on everything, but it means that we can at least honor our differences, and that we can be able to work together with a good and loving spirit. This is so important, for God cannot work in a church that is marred by division. The devil loves to put enmity between brothers and sisters, and he looks for every opportunity to drive wedges among the members of the church and between the members and the ministry. We must always work to keep a degree of unity within the Body of Christ.

The Promise of the Father

Quickly and unexpectedly, a sound came from heaven like a violent storm was approaching, and it came in and filled the whole house where the 120 had gathered. They saw cloven tongues that appeared like fire sitting upon each of their heads as God poured out His Holy Spirit and they all began to speak in other languages as the Holy Spirit gave them the ability to do so. This was the Promise of the Father that Jesus said He would send upon them. (Please see chapter 2 of this book for a complete explanation on this subject).

The prophet Joel prophesied of this great promise of the outpouring of God's Spirit upon all flesh approximately 800 years before it happened. The Apostle Peter also referred to this prophecy during his sermon on Pentecost Sunday (*Acts 2:16-18*) when relating the display of worship and praise and the sound of the speaking in tongues of the 120 believers who had just received the Gift of the Holy Ghost.

> *And ye shall know that I am in the midst of Israel, and that I am the LORD your God, and none else: and my people shall never be ashamed. And it shall come to pass afterward, that I will pour out my spirit upon all flesh; and your sons and your daughters shall prophesy, your old men shall dream dreams, your young men shall see visions: (Joel 2:27-28)*

This was the birth of the New Testament Church that happened almost two thousand years ago. God miraculously put His Holy Spirit inside of those New Testament believers and when He did, they spoke in other tongues as was recorded in Acts 2:1-4. And this wasn't the only time this would happen. You will read about it in Acts Chapters 10 and 19 and in 1 Corinthians Chapter 14. In the other instances, the wind and cloven tongues of fire do not appear, just the speaking in tongues. Today as people receive this same Holy Spirit, just like the one hundred and twenty did on that first Pentecost Sunday, they speak in tongues. Now I know that this may not be your experience, and I realize that many do not believe that this is possible today. But please do not close the book just yet. Just go with me a little further.

We often have visiting ministers come to minister in our services. Sometimes we have missionaries who have been working in foreign lands coming back into the United States to raise their funds to go back to the mission field for the next four years. It is interesting when we have an opportunity to speak with the missionaries about people receiving the Holy Ghost in their native country. We are told that sometimes they speak in tongues in English, having never learned the language. When asked what they are saying, they replied, they are glorifying God.

I was working in a Spanish church for a few years, in North Charleston South Carolina, and one Sunday a family came into the sanctuary. The family was African American, and none of them spoke Spanish. That day one of the family members came to the altar and received the Gift of the Holy Ghost, and when he did, he spoke in Spanish.

Many times, during a church service people may speak in tongues for personal edification (*1 Corinthians 14: 2, 4, 14, 28, 39*). Once while a friend of mine was speaking in tongues in a service, a woman who was in the pew in front of him heard him speaking. After the service was over the woman approached my friend and asked him if he spoke Hebrew. He said, "No, I don't know Hebrew, why do you ask me that?" She told him that while he was praying, he was speaking fluent Hebrew. When he asked her what he was saying, she replied, "The peace of God be upon you, the peace of God be upon you."

It is also so amazing to watch a young boy of about nine years old speak in tongues as he receives the Holy Ghost with nobody instructing or prompting him to do so. I've seen it happen more than once. A person comes to the altar area and begins to cry out to God, and in a moment, without anyone coaching him, he begins to speak in an unknown tongue. I once witnessed a woman who, from the start of the service, could not stop weeping. Her tears flowed throughout the service including during the preaching. When the call to come to the altar was made, this woman came, lifted her hands, and was speaking in other tongues. That is not the way it happens with everyone, but when it happens like that, it is a beautiful thing to see.

What Meaneth This?

> *And there were dwelling at Jerusalem Jews, devout men, out of every nation under heaven. Now when this was noised abroad, the multitude came together, and were confounded, because that every man heard them speak in his own language. And they were all amazed and marvelled, saying one to another, Behold, are not all these which speak Galilaeans? And how hear we every man in our own tongue, wherein we were born? Parthians, and Medes, and Elamites, and the dwellers in Mesopotamia, and in Judaea, and Cappadocia, in Pontus, and Asia, Phrygia, and Pamphylia, in Egypt, and in the parts of Libya about Cyrene, and strangers of Rome, Jews and proselytes, Cretes and Arabians, we do hear them speak in our tongues the wonderful works of God. And they were all amazed, and were in doubt, saying one to another, What meaneth this? (Acts 2:5-12)*

There are at least two major responses that take place when people hear the preaching of the Word or during a supernatural event orchestrated by God like the one in Acts 2. One is acceptance or belief in what is heard or seen, and the other is disbelief, which usually results in mocking, or ridiculing as opposition rears its ugly head and conflicts arise. This was no different on the first Pentecost Sunday when God poured out His Holy Spirit upon those 120 believers as the New Testament Church was born.

This outpouring of the Holy Spirit happened around 9 am. The quiet streets of Jerusalem were filled with the ecstatic sounds of worship and praises to Almighty God. This "noise" caused a crowd to form, and as they arrived, they began to hear the 120 speaking different languages, each one hearing a language in their native tongue. There were about 15-17 languages that were represented by this crowd, and knowing that these Galileans did not comprehend their language, they said, "How hear we every man in our own tongue, wherein we were born?" (*Acts 2:8*) And what were they speaking? They said they were speaking the "Wonderful works of God" (*Acts 2:12*). The scripture says that some were "all amazed," and others were in doubt as to what happened exclaiming, *"What meaneth this?"*

The subject of tongues was a question in 33 A.D., and it is still a question today. Speaking in tongues is also known as "glossolalia." This is a supernatural event whereby one speaks in a language he does not know or has never been taught, a language unknown to him; he does so as the Spirit of God gives him the utterance. The Complete Bible Library says:

> *The 120 spoke in real languages which were actually understood by a variety of people from a variety of places. This gave witness to the universality of the Gift and to the universality and unity of the Church.* [4]

Some authorities believe that the tongues in Acts 2 were given to preach the gospel to the different peoples that came to see what was taking place that morning. But the Bible never says that tongues were given for this purpose. In fact, when we study the other occurrences in the Book of Acts where groups of people received the Holy Ghost and spoke with tongues, it becomes obvious that they were not preaching to anyone.

What is the purpose of preaching? It is to proclaim the Good News of the Gospel to a lost world! The crowd only gathered where the believers were that morning because they heard a commotion. The 120 were speaking in tongues well before the crowd ever arrived. What would have been the purpose of the 120 preaching the Gospel when there was no one there to hear it? Also, the Bible says that they were speaking the "wonderful works of God." They were not preaching doctrine or telling people what they needed to do to be saved. And then, why did Peter get up and answer the question, "What Meaneth This?" speaking in the one language that everyone could understand? Or do we believe that Peter spoke in 17 different languages that day? No, this speaking in tongues was the evidence that these 120 had received the Gift of the Holy Ghost. We will see this as we continue on in the Book of Acts. The scripture never says that the 120 were preaching the Gospel.

Some have even charged today that speaking in tongues is of the devil. This is an extremely dangerous charge that cannot be proven in the scripture. First, scripture says that the sound came from heaven. Secondly, it was the "Holy Spirit" that gave them the ability to speak in tongues. Thirdly, what were the people doing? They were magnifying God and proclaiming His wonderful works. Now, wherever in scripture do we see the devil magnifying or proclaiming the good works of God?

When we attribute to the devil something that is of God, we stand in the danger of blaspheming the Holy Ghost. This is what happened in Mark 3:

> *And he called them unto him, and said unto them in parables, How can Satan cast out Satan? And if a kingdom be divided against itself, that kingdom cannot stand. And if a house be divided against itself, that house cannot stand. And if Satan rise up against himself, and be divided, he cannot stand, but hath an end. No man can enter into a strong man's house, and spoil his goods, except he will first bind the strong man; and then he will spoil his house. Verily I say unto you, All sins shall be forgiven unto the sons of men, and blasphemies wherewith soever they shall blaspheme: But he that shall blaspheme against the Holy Ghost hath never forgiveness, but is in danger of eternal damnation: Because they said, He hath an unclean spirit. (Mark 3:23-30)*

The scribes were saying that Jesus was a devil and that he casts out devils by the prince of devils. That would make Jesus in league with the devil, which is not true and is blasphemy. Speaking in tongues is never depicted in the scripture as being something attributed to the devil, but it is always used in relationship to God. Satan can mimic or counterfeit something of God, but a Holy Ghost filled Christian can discern the difference of the spirit.

There is another misunderstanding about tongues and its usage. So many commentators and biblical scholars teach of the speaking in tongues on the Day of Pentecost in the Book of Acts as the "Gift of Tongues." However, that is not correct. When people received the Holy Ghost in the Book of Acts and spoke in tongues, they received the "Gift of the Holy Ghost." This is true in Acts 2, 10, 19, and there is good reason to believe it is the same in chapter 8. This speaking in tongues is the evidence that someone has received the *gift of the Holy Ghost*. Notice in the Book of Acts that there is no instruction on the usage of the tongues in these chapters. That is because it is not the *gift of Tongues*, it is the *gift of the Holy Ghost* that one receives as a part of the New Birth experience of John 3: 3, 5.

In 1 Corinthians 12 through 14 the Apostle Paul wrote to the Church about the Gifts of the Spirit:

> *Now concerning spiritual gifts, brethren, I would not have you ignorant. Ye know that ye were Gentiles, carried away unto these dumb idols, even as ye were led. Wherefore I give you to understand, that no man speaking by the Spirit of God calleth Jesus accursed: and that no man can say that Jesus is the Lord, but by the Holy Ghost. Now there are diversities of gifts, but the same Spirit. And there are differences of administrations, but the same Lord. And there are diversities of operations, but it is the same God which worketh all in all. But the manifestation of the Spirit is given to every man to profit withal. For to one is given by the Spirit the word of wisdom; to another the word of knowledge by the same Spirit; To another faith by the same Spirit; to another the gifts of healing by the same Spirit; To another the working of miracles; to another prophecy; to another discerning of spirits; to another divers kinds of tongues; to another the interpretation of tongues: But all these worketh that one and the selfsame Spirit, dividing to every man severally as he will. (1 Corinthians 12:1-11)*

When you read 1 Corinthians 14, you will see that there is much instruction on how these two gifts—*Divers kinds of tongues and the Interpretation of Tongues*—work together in order for the Church to be edified. In fact, the edification of the Church is the reason for all of the Gifts of the Spirit. Notice the following scriptures:

- *For he that speaketh in an unknown tongue speaketh not unto men, but unto God: for no man understandeth him; howbeit in the spirit he speaketh mysteries... He that speaketh in an unknown tongue edifieth himself; but he that prophesieth edifieth the church. I would that ye all spake with tongues, but rather that ye prophesied: for greater is he that prophesieth than he that speaketh with tongues, except he interpret, that the church may receive edifying. (1 Corinthians 14: 2, 4-5)*
- *For if I pray in an unknown tongue, my spirit prayeth, but my understanding is unfruitful. What is it then? I will pray with the spirit, and I will pray with the understanding also: I will sing with the spirit, and I will sing with the understanding also. (1 Corinthians 14:14-15)*
- *If any man speak in an unknown tongue, let it be by two, or at the most by three, and that by course; and let one interpret. But if there be no interpreter, let him keep silence in the church; and let him speak to himself, and to God. (1 Corinthians 14:27-28)*
- *Wherefore, brethren, covet to prophesy, and forbid not to speak with tongues. Let all things be done decently and in order. (1 Corinthians 14:39-40)*

It is evident in these scriptures that there was a definite place in the early Church for speaking in tongues. Tongues is something that was used in prayer for personal edification (*1 Corinthians 14:5*), and it was also used during Church services (*1 Corinthians 14: 5, 27-28*).

These scriptures indicate that there was a certain way in which the "Gift of Divers Kinds of Tongues" and the "Gift of the Interpretation of Tongues" operate. In order for the tongues to be interpreted there must be someone there to operate in the Gift of Interpretation of Tongues. Otherwise, the Church could not be edified, and the edification of the Church is the reason for the gifts. In that case, the person who is operating in the *gift of divers kinds of Tongues* should not speak out loud but pray to himself.

All of this was written because the Corinthians were misusing the gifts and as the Apostle Paul wrote at the end of Chapter 14, "Let all things be done decently and in order." It is incredible to believe that the Holy Spirit would have inspired three chapters—Chapters 12 through 14--in 1 Corinthians on the Gifts of the Spirit if it was something that the Church in later centuries would not have needed. I've also read how many commentators say that Paul states that not all speak in tongues. This is referring to 1 Corinthians 12:29-30:

> *Are all apostles? are all prophets? are all teachers? are all workers of miracles? Have all the gifts of healing? do all speak with tongues? do all interpret? (1 Corinthians 12:29-30)*

In the context of this chapter, Paul is speaking about the operation of the Gifts of the Spirit, not what happens when someone receives the Gift of the Holy Ghost. While we believe that when someone receives the Holy Ghost they speak in an unknown tongue as evidence that they have received it, we also believe that not every believer receives the *gift of divers kinds of Tongues* or *the interpretation of Tongues*. All nine Gifts of the Spirit found in 1 Corinthians Chapter 12 are given to the Church by God. In the last verse, Paul says that we should "covet to prophesy, and forbid not to speak with tongues." Or as the NLT says, "be eager to prophesy, and don't forbid speaking in tongues."

God Performs Miracles Today

There are some Bible commentators who believe that speaking in tongues, the Gifts of the Spirit, and healing and miracles disappeared with the death of the apostles. I question such conclusions. If this is the same church that Jesus purchased with His blood, and if He has given us the same Spirit that He gave to the First Century Church, then why would the gifts have stopped working? Do we need the benefits of the gifts any less than the Church of the First Century? Did the early church live in a darker time than we do? More Importantly, where does the scripture say that healings, miracles, and tongues have stopped working in the Church?

The 28th Chapter of Acts is the final chapter of that book. In the chapter, Paul is bitten by a venomous snake, yet he does not die to the great amazement of the people of the island of Melita. A little while later the Apostle prays for healing for the leader of the people. He is healed and then the island people start bringing their sick folk to Paul for healing also. What a way to end that book of action and power! This certainly does not sound like a church that the Spirit of God has stopped displaying His miraculous power in. The Book of Acts has no ending and we are the continuation of that book today. We are the Spirit filled Apostolic Church of the 21st Century and we need the demonstration of the power of the Holy Spirit if we are to deliver our world from the power of darkness.

On the mission fields today, reports of miracles happen quite often. Cancers healed, blind eyes opened, the dumb made to speak and many other kinds of miracles abound. In my previous home church, a young boy was diagnosed with a brain tumor. His mother asked for prayer after a mid-week service in which I preached a message called, "Sometimes You Just Need a Miracle." We prayed for him and about a week later, after a second MRI, the mother told us that the doctors couldn't find the tumor. God had miraculously healed him, and today, this young man is serving in our armed forces! Praise God!

A woman I know in our church in New York was born with a rare congenital birth defect which caused a loss of hearing resulting from structural abnormalities in the middle and inner ear. She was born without a Eustachian tube and the Doctors concluded that nothing could be done to correct it. She had lived many years without being able to hear in her right ear.

During a service, when we had a visiting minister preaching for us, our sister went up to pray for her healing in her ear. She said as she was praying, she felt a push of air blow against her eardrum from inside of her ear. Then her right ear made a loud pop, and it started to crackle. Praise God, she could hear for the first time in her right ear!

God has performed a miracle in my own life. My family was involved in a terrible car accident. My two sons, along with myself, were injured in the crash as our car flipped over several times and came to a stop on the roof of the car. My boys were not severely injured, so they were treated and stayed overnight in the hospital. I was more severely injured. The left side of my face had been torn away when it collided with the road as the car flipped over and continued to spin on its roof. Most of the skin on the left side of my face was gone, including three-fourths of my eyelid. My left cheekbone and orbital socket had been worn down by a severe form of road rash. A good part of the miracle was that with all the damage to my face and around my eye, my eye was not damaged and no bones in my skull were broken.

I had surgery early in the morning about 2 a.m. The doctor had to make a new eyelid for me from a skin graft because a good part of my eyelid was torn away in the accident. The doctor told my wife to let me know ahead of time that I probably would lose the sight in the eye because I would not be able to blink or close my eye completely due to the damaged nerves and muscles. When she told me this, I immediately said, "No way. God will not let this happen to me." When the doctor removed my stitches a week later, the first thing I asked him was, "Can I blink my eye?" I had faith to believe I could. He replied, "Well, go ahead and try." I tried, and it blinked! The doctor was amazed and said, "Do that again." I did and he was astounded and became very excited. He told me that he had no medical explanation for what I was doing because the muscles and the nerves were all damaged. When I told him that my God had performed a miracle, he said, "Well, I would be thrown out of the medical profession if I admitted that, but I have no other explanation for what you are doing." Now 36 year later, my vision is still very good in my left eye, and sometimes I see better out of it than I do out of my right eye. Glory be to God!!

The following is a miracle God performed for a young girl at the church I attend in North Carolina: In October of 2019, a young girl slipped and bumped her arm on a car door while getting out. This should've been only a bruise at most. She was upset but was not complaining of pain. She just kept saying that her "arm felt weird." At her insistence, her parents took her to urgent care to get an x-ray. The provider they saw was shocked when the x-ray showed she had fractured her humerus (*one of the strongest bones in the body*). The reason it had fractured with such a slight impact was because of an abnormal bone lesion.

What they didn't tell the parents at that time is that the lesion had the appearance of a malignant (*cancerous*) bone tumor. Their findings were stated as "cells of ill-defined margins." The family was sent home from urgent care with the young girl's arm set in a temporary cast. The parents were told to follow-up with an orthopedic doctor. The young girl's mother, being a nurse, knew the possibility of this kind of mass being cancerous. Our church family and friends from all over began to pray. The first miraculous thing happened when the hospital performed an emergency MRI and they found that the mass was benign. The mother said, "I know that was God. Every doctor that saw her x-ray was very concerned that the lesion looked cancerous." The second miraculous thing was that although a fractured humerus is typically a very painful injury, the young girl never had any pain, much less stiffness. She spent 7-8 weeks with her arm bent at 90 degrees, and as soon as her cast was removed, she had full range of motion. This young 10-year-old girl has developed great faith in God. She told her mother that, "I know you always told me that God can heal, but now I know for myself." What an awesome thing to come from what could have been a great tragedy. God is Great!

I can remember another miracle God performed when I was just a young Christian. A work friend of my mom's was in a severe car accident and was badly injured. As it turned out, the woman was paralyzed from the waist down. One day the woman came to church and after the sermon, the visiting minister asked if anyone wanted to be healed. The woman replied that she wanted to be healed, and after prayer, the preacher told her to rise out of the wheelchair. She not only got up from the chair, but she walked all around the sanctuary. Her son walked in and said, "Is that my mother? She hasn't walked in years!" But she did that night. Thank God for performing miracles in our day!

While I was serving as an assistant pastor, my wife and I became quite close with a young couple who had recently come to the Lord. We began to mentor them and teach them a home bible study, and our relationship with them became very close. They had struggled with infertility after the birth of their son but had longed for another child. After several miscarriages, they were beginning to give up hope of ever having another child. That's when they had their first miracle, a pregnancy was confirmed.

At thirteen weeks into the pregnancy, a high-risk specialist told this young mother that her pregnancy would have to be terminated. Confirmed by MRI and Ultrasound, the fetus had implanted itself in a part of the uterus where it would be unable to grow and develop (a cornual pregnancy). In this type of pregnancy, the mother is at great risk also of a uterine rupture and severe bleeding, exacerbated by the fact of the mother being on blood thinning medication. Devastated by this report, they asked us and the church to pray.

One week later, the mother was scheduled for a 3-D Ultrasound to check the position of the fetus. That's when God gave them their second miracle. The baby had moved its way to a viable position in the uterus! This baby would now have room to grow! Any one would think that this was enough, God had showed His mercy and power in these two miracles. But God wasn't finished yet.

The couple was told at 20 weeks, that this was a very high-risk pregnancy. The mother was at risk of premature labor, due to a shortened cervix, and was put on bedrest. During the next several weeks she was in and out of the hospital. They were informed of all the possible complications that a "very preterm" baby could be born with. The goal of the doctors was for her to make it until at least 32 weeks of pregnancy. At exactly 30 weeks, her water broke with contractions 2-3 minutes apart. With medications, the doctors were able to delay the birth for only another 3 days. At around 2 am, the doctors became quite concerned about the baby's heart rate and lack of movement. An emergency C-section was preformed and tiny Isabella was born. She weighed only 3.2 pounds and was 15 inches long. Miraculously she was breathing well on her own and did not require oxygen which is amazing considering that she was born before 32 weeks when the lungs would not have been fully formed.

Tiny Isabella spent 47 days in the NICU, overcoming many medical problems associated with premature infants. At one point, her weight went down to 2.4 pounds, but our miracle working God was working in her, and in the lives of her parents. They never lost faith, they never lost hope! During those difficult months while she was hospitalized, her parents learned to fast and pray. They learned to trust in God. Isabella is a beautiful little girl now, living with her family, praising God for their miracle child.

This next narrative is not about a physical healing but a spiritual and emotional miracle. This is a story about a man I've known for twenty-two years. He started to come to church with a great desire to seek God. He was suffering from constant depression and sadness. He was in his early twenty's when I met him and at that time he explained to me how he had visited psychiatrists and psychologists from the age of seven years old. As a child he constantly wondered why there was so much sadness, hurt, and suffering in the world. Anti-depressants were his daily norm. He just accepted the fact that depression would be a part of the rest of his life. But this young man was hungry for God. He wanted that peace that passes all understanding that the Bible talks about.

One cold January night he was invited to go to a home fellowship/prayer meeting. The person leading the meeting prayed for him and told him to ask God for whatever he wanted. He said to himself in a quiet voice, "I don't want to feel depressed anymore." As soon as he began to pray that prayer, he felt the weight of depression instantly lift from him. The depression was gone! The sadness was gone! And in an act of faith, he threw away all of his anti-depressant medication (disclaimer: I am not encouraging nor endorsing anyone to throw away or stop taking medication). Now at the age of forty-four, he is happily married with two wonderful children, continuing in the grace and love of God. He tells everyone he meets that even though sadness and hurt may come, we don't have to live in defeat and depression because Jesus can take it all away.

Each of these miracles had a tremendous impact on my life. These are firsthand accounts because I know each one personally, and I saw with my own eyes the miraculous hand of God at work. Glory to God. Thank God for performing miracles in the 21st Century!

Some may still remark that miracles and healings don't happen as often as they did in the Bible. But where are they getting their information? Every day we live and breathe, it is a miracle. How many times has God provided for you? Is that not a miracle? I'm reminded of the Old Testament story in 1 Kings 17 of a widow who had a handful of meal and a small vial of oil. Because she obeyed the prophet and gave all she had, she and her son lived. Each day, God provided the same amount of meal and oil. It doesn't say she became rich and all her problems went away. Yet was it any less of a miracle? God's provision in our lives is truly miraculous. Let us pray that God opens our eyes to the miracles that occur daily.

Will Tongues Cease?

God in His mercy still performs miracles today and speaking in tongues today as evidence of receiving the Holy Spirit is a miraculous gift in and of itself. There are those who even say that this "glossolalia" ceased to exist at some unknown time in the past and is not for our generation. They use a scripture in 1 Corinthians 13 to support their argument. Read this passage. Is that really what the scripture is stating?

> *Charity never faileth: but whether there be prophecies, they shall fail; whether there be tongues, they shall cease; whether there be knowledge, it shall vanish away. For we know in part, and we prophesy in part. But when that which is perfect is come, then that which is in part shall be done away.* (1 Corinthians 13:8-10)

This scripture certainly states that speaking in tongues will cease at some point, but when will that happen? The scripture says in verse 9 that, "For we know in part, and we prophesy in part." Is this scripture telling us that tongues have already ceased? John MacArthur writes in his commentary on 1 Corinthians 13, "Paul considers tongues already to have stopped, because that gift is not mentioned after verse 8." [5]

It may be possible to have partial knowledge, and we can understand how we can prophesy in part, but how do you speak in tongues in part? You either speak or you don't speak, and that is probably why the scripture doesn't include tongues in that verse.

Now the passage states that knowledge will vanish away. Knowledge has certainly not vanished away yet. Just think about how quickly technology advances and our phones, computers, etc. become out of date within a few years. Instead of vanishing away, knowledge has been increasing every day. In Daniel 12, the scripture tells us this will be in the end times.

> *But thou, O Daniel, shut up the words, and seal the book, even to the time of the end: many shall run to and fro, and knowledge shall be increased.* (Daniel 12:4)

This scripture is so spot on in the 21st Century. Knowledge in so many fields is growing by leaps and bounds, especially in the scientific, electronic, and IT fields. Things that were not possible just forty or fifty years ago are possible today, helping us to understand even how some of the prophesies of the Bible can come to pass today.

What about prophecy? Do we have complete understanding of all prophecy? Has every prophetic word or passage in the Bible come to pass? No, they haven't. There are many prophetic utterances in both the Old Testament and the New Testament that are still awaiting fulfillment. So, there is still the need for knowledge and prophecy. When will they cease?

The scripture goes on to say in 1 Corinthians 13:10, "When that which is perfect is come, then that which is in part will be done away." Has "That which is perfect" come already? It is not logical to assume that knowledge, prophecy, and tongues have ceased until the time of perfection has come. Are we living in a time of perfection? No! That which is perfect has not yet come – it will not come until sin has been completely defeated, and we are all living in our new home in God's great Kingdom of Heaven. The passage is speaking of a future day when we will be forever with the Lord. In that day there will be no need for prophecy, for it will have all been fulfilled. There will be no need of knowledge, for we will know all things. There also will be no need to speak in tongues, for we will all have been redeemed. As the Apostle Paul says: "For now we see through a glass, darkly; but then face to face: now I know in part; but then shall I know even as also I am known" *(1 Corinthians 13:12)*. And Sproul says of Pentecost:

> *The day of Pentecost was that moment in redemptive history when God unlocked the power of the Holy Spirit and gave it to His Church, not just for those who were gathered there, but to the Church of every age and to every Christian throughout time. The wind, that fire, is as much for us today as it was for those gathered in the upper room."* [6]

The following quotations are taken from a book named, "What Meaneth This?" by Carl Brumback. In his book he quotes historians and church fathers down through the ages to show us that speaking in tongues has definitely not ceased but has continued to go on as believers receive the gift of the Holy Ghost.

- According to the Encyclopedia Britannica, the glossolalia *'recurs in Christian revivals of every age.'*

- Under Second and Third Centuries
- There is a quote from the "History of the Apostolic Church", Book 1, Sec. 55 by Philip Schaff: *The speaking with tongues, however, was not confined to the day of Pentecost...We find traces of it still in the second and third centuries.*
- Augustine (354-430) wrote: *We still do what the apostles did when they laid hands on the Samaritans and called down the Holy Spirit on them by laying on of hands. It is expected that converts should speak with new tongues.*
- Under Fifth Century to Reformation
- *But even in the Dark Ages God gave some gracious revivals. From the Twelfth to the Fifteenth Century there were revivals in southern Europe in which many spoke in tongues. Foremost among these revivalists were the Waldenses and Albigenses.*
- Under Reformation to Twentieth Century
- Encyclopedia Britannica (Vol. 22, p283) tells of tongues *'among the Jensenists and early Quakers, the converts of Wesley and Whitefield, the persecuted Protestants of the Cevennes, and the Irvingites.*
- Chrysostom tells us: *'Whoever was baptized in apostolic day, he straightway spake with tongues; they at once received the Spirit; not that they saw the Spirit, for He is invisible, but God's grace bestowed some sensible proof of His energy. It thus made manifest to them that were without that it was the Spirit in the very person speaking.'* [7]

This is only a few of the many quotations that are found showing that tongues have been present down through the centuries and certainly have not ceased. And the reason that so many don't receive it is because they don't believe it! What a miraculous gift God has given us! Even though we live in an imperfect world, we can have God's Spirit inside of us, and it's just as much for us today as it was in the book of Acts!

Final Thoughts

Until the time when God comes to take His Church home, the True Church will continue exactly as it began – people being filled with the Holy Ghost, speaking in other tongues as the Spirit gives the utterance. Miracles and healings abound, all through the power of the Holy Ghost. It began on the Day of Pentecost (*A.D.33*) and continues until this day – God's Spirit is being poured out "upon all flesh." Research shows that each week there are approximately thousands worldwide receiving the Holy Ghost by speaking with other tongues.[8] Darrel Bock in his commentary addresses this topic:

> *The descent of the Spirit on the day of Pentecost comes with indications that God has acted...Acts is showing God at work. As is often the case when God works, many who see it have no clue what is taking place, making light of it. No one should be surprised at such a variety of reactions when God works. Some do not see what God is doing even after it is explained.* [9]

My wife and I both received the Holy Ghost and were baptized in Jesus name on Sept. 23, 1975, in Schenectady, New York. This was the greatest day of our lives. After repenting of our sins, we received the Holy Ghost and were baptized in the only name whereby we must be saved! What we felt was indescribable! Our sins had been forgiven; our burdens were lifted. We both felt so free and clean. I remember feeling like I was floating on air, and my feet weren't touching the ground though they actually were. My wife described it as feeling like a fountain was flowing out of her! We felt such a peace that could not be explained.

I used to have a really foul mouth. I worked alongside other men in a warehouse where all kind of foul words were used, and I was one of the worst. But after receiving the Holy Ghost, it was as if God took an eraser and ran it across my tongue. I didn't even have to cautiously watch what I said. I just didn't use bad language anymore. It was a miracle!

Not only did I stop cursing, I immediately stopped drinking alcohol, which I used to do every Tuesday night when I bowled in my work league. I used to get quite drunk every Tuesday and then go to work at midnight where I was required to operate heavy machinery. Often, I was told to go sleep it off. The guys used to call me "TNT," the Tuesday Night Terror. But after receiving the Holy Ghost, I didn't even want to go into the bar anymore. I also smoked four packs of cigarettes daily. I stopped smoking cold turkey and I have never smoked again. I received a tremendous love for the Word of God which I used to devour every spare moment I had. Go ahead and mock me if you will, but please don't tell me that speaking in tongues doesn't exist today. It exists, it's God-given, and it's life changing.

In these last days, we need to pray and ask God to open our eyes. When speaking of God's miraculous outpouring of His Holy Spirit, some are amazed and desire to receive it, but some mockingly say, "What Meaneth This?" His miraculous works are all around us. Let us not turn a blind eye to them. As it was on the Day of Pentecost, so it is today.

4
PETER'S FIRST GOSPEL SERMON

I was in the 8th grade when I joined a speech club in my elementary school. I can't remember why I would have joined such a club as I didn't like speaking in front of other people. And wouldn't you know, to make it even worse, I was asked to be the one to represent our school in a speech contest. I have no idea why I was chosen because I was always the shy little kid who never wanted to answer questions in class because I was so self-conscious that my answers would be wrong and everybody would laugh at me.

I was given a speech by Adlai Stevenson that I was to memorize. The speech was to be about five minutes long. My teacher had me attend different classes to practice giving the speech. I had to stand before the Monsignor, who is the head of the rectory (the place where the parish priests live) to give my speech. He then critiqued my speech and tried to help me deliver it with more emphasis. Needless to say, I was very uneasy doing this. My hands became cold as ice, as the nervous feeling of butterflies filled my stomach. I couldn't wait for it to be over, and I really didn't care if I won the contest or not.

Finally, the day arrived and all six contestants were told the rules and given the order in which we would give our speech. I think I was the fifth person to speak. My stomach was in knots, and I was hoping I didn't forget my words or stumble over any part of the speech. I did the best I could do, but I didn't win. I don't even think I came in second place. I can't even relate the horrific fear I had in speaking to an auditorium full of adults with everybody's eyes looking directly at me.

On the Day of Pentecost when the crowd was mocking and wondering what was going on, the Apostle Peter, an unlearned fisherman, stood up and addressed probably somewhere between 5000-7000 people (the Bible doesn't say how big the crowd was). I wonder if his heart was pounding like mine was. Peter was not the kind of man who was used to giving speeches, but he did have the Holy Ghost, and when he stood up and preached the first Apostolic Message, he hit it out of the ballpark! Three thousand souls were saved on that first Sunday of the New Apostolic Church.

> *Others mocking said, These men are full of new wine. But Peter, standing up with the eleven, lifted up his voice, and said unto them, Ye men of Judaea, and all ye that dwell at Jerusalem, be this known unto you, and hearken to my words: For these are not drunken, as ye suppose, seeing it is but the third hour of the day. But this is that which was spoken by the prophet Joel; And it shall come to pass in the last days, saith God, I will pour out of my Spirit upon all flesh: and your sons and your daughters shall prophesy, and your young men shall see visions, and your old men shall dream dreams: And on my servants and on my handmaidens I will pour out in those days of my Spirit; and they shall prophesy: And I will shew wonders in heaven above, and signs in the earth beneath; blood, and fire, and vapour of smoke: The sun shall be turned into darkness, and the moon into blood, before that great and notable day of the Lord come: And it shall come to pass, that whoso-ever shall call on the name of the Lord shall be saved. Ye men of Israel, hear these words; Jesus of Nazareth, a man approved of God among you by miracles and wonders and signs, which God did by him in the midst of you, as ye yourselves also know: Him, being delivered by the determinate counsel and foreknowledge of God, ye have taken, and by wicked hands have crucified and slain: Whom God hath*

raised up, having loosed the pains of death: because it was not possible that he should be holden of it. For David speaketh concerning him, I foresaw the Lord always before my face, for he is on my right hand, that I should not be moved: Therefore did my heart rejoice, and my tongue was glad; moreover also my flesh shall rest in hope: Because thou wilt not leave my soul in hell, neither wilt thou suffer thine Holy One to see corruption. Thou hast made known to me the ways of life; thou shalt make me full of joy with thy countenance. Men and brethren, let me freely speak unto you of the patriarch David, that he is both dead and buried, and his sepulchre is with us unto this day. Therefore being a prophet, and knowing that God had sworn with an oath to him, that of the fruit of his loins, according to the flesh, he would raise up Christ to sit on his throne; He seeing this before spake of the resurrection of Christ, that his soul was not left in hell, neither his flesh did see corruption. This Jesus hath God raised up, whereof we all are witnesses. Therefore being by the right hand of God exalted and having received of the Father the promise of the Holy Ghost, he hath shed forth this, which ye now see and hear. For David is not ascended into the heavens: but he saith himself, The LORD said unto my Lord, Sit thou on my right hand, Until I make thy foes thy footstool. Therefore let all the house of Israel know assuredly, that God hath made that same Jesus, whom ye have crucified, both Lord and Christ. Now when they heard this, they were pricked in their heart, and said unto Peter and to the rest of the apostles, Men and brethren, what shall we do? Then Peter said unto them, Repent, and be baptized every one of you in the name of Jesus Christ for the remission of sins, and ye shall receive the gift of the Holy Ghost. For the promise is unto you, and to your children, and to all that are afar off, even as many as the Lord our God shall call. And with many other words did he testify and exhort, saying, Save yourselves from this untoward generation. Then they that gladly received his word were baptized: and the same day there were added unto them about three thousand souls. (Acts 2:13-41)

We Are Not Drunk as Ye Suppose

Some who came to see what was going on that Pentecost morning were amazed, some were in doubt, and others mocked, accusing the 120 to be drunk with wine. However, it seems that everyone was moved by what they witnessed in one way or another. Peter, taking advantage of the situation, stood up, and filled with the Holy Ghost, began to speak to the people. He argued, "How can you think that these people are drunk with wine when it is only 9 o'clock in the morning?" No, we are not drunken as ye suppose but <u>this</u> (*what you are witnessing*) is <u>that</u> (*the fulfillment of Joel's prophecy*)." Joel prophesied about the outpouring of the Holy Ghost 800 years prior to that day. Peter exhorts the crowd, reminding them of the prophecy:

> *And it shall come to pass in the last days, saith God, I will pour out of my Spirit upon all flesh: and your sons and your daughters shall prophesy, and your young men shall see visions, and your old men shall dream dreams: And on my servants and on my handmaidens I will pour out in those days of my Spirit; and they shall prophesy: And I will shew wonders in heaven above, and signs in the earth beneath; blood, and fire, and vapour of smoke: The sun shall be turned into darkness, and the moon into blood, before that great and notable day of the Lord come: And it shall come to pass, that whosoever shall call on the name of the Lord shall be saved. (Acts 2:17-21)*

It is interesting to note that Peter did not quote Joel exactly. Joel started by saying, "And it shall come to pass afterward," but Peter attached this prophecy to the last days when he said, "And it shall come to pass *in the last days*, saith God." However, the entire prophecy was not fulfilled on the first Pentecost Sunday, for verses 17-18 are the beginning of the last days. We are now in the year 2023, and the first part of this prophecy has continued to be fulfilled as the Church Age has existed now for about 2,000 years. We are living in the last days and God is still pouring out His Spirit all over the world as a witness to this prophetic fulfillment. However, the next three verses (*18-20*) are still awaiting fulfillment, and the time spoken of here is the Day of the Lord when God shall pour out His wrath upon the world of the ungodly. The NIV New Application Commentary further explains:

What the people are witnessing is the 'beginning' of the last days, when people of all types and ages will prophecy (vv 17b-18). At the 'end' of the last days will be cosmic disturbances.....which will herald 'the great and glorious day of the Lord' (v.20b) – the day of judgment at the end of the world. [1]

So, from Joel's prophecy to that first Pentecost Sunday and until the Day of the Lord, even in 2023, whosoever will call on the name of the Lord will find salvation in Jesus Christ. That is something to be excited about! The promise of salvation is for you and for me and for "whosoever will."

Peters First Message

Having their attention, Peter then began to preach to the people. All that were in the audience that day were Jews, and Peter's sermon revolved around Jesus and His ministry. He pointed out that Jesus was a man approved by God that lived among them, and His ministry was defined by the miracles, wonders, and signs which He did right in front of their eyes. They knew Him and heard His teachings. They saw Him perform great miracles that had never been done in Israel before, like opening blinded eyes. Jesus came to give them a glimpse of what living life in His Kingdom would be all about. Peter took this opportunity to let them know that it wasn't over. There was still hope, but it was also a call to action. As Darrell Bock explains in his commentary: "At the end of his speech, Peter will use the coming of judgment as an appeal for the people to repent and thereby experience the blessings of the new era." [2]

Peter's message of hope and conviction continued. He reminded the crowd that they crucified Him! (*Acts 2:36*) This was not necessarily said of them personally, but Israel as a nation had rejected Jesus, and in that sense, they were all guilty of crucifying Him. Peter also mentioned that it was the "Determinate counsel and foreknowledge of God" (*Acts 2:23*) that had led Jesus to the cross. In other words, it was God's will that determined that Jesus would go to the cross. This was God's plan from the beginning when He told Eve that the seed of the woman would crush the head of the serpent, but in the process, His heel would be bruised. This bruising of the heel happened at Calvary in approximately 32 AD.

Peter exclaimed that Jesus may have died, but death could not hold Him! The Spirit of Almighty God, which dwelt in Jesus bodily (*Colossians 3:9*), entered back into His lifeless body three days after His death. God had raised Him because death had no right or claim to His body. Death is a consequence of sin. The scripture says, "The soul that sinneth, it shall die" (*Ezekiel 18:4*). Sin has affected every human soul born into this world because we all are born with the nature of sin. However, because Jesus did not have a sinful human nature, and since throughout His life He never sinned, death could not hold Him. He is the only human being that was completely without sin.

Next, Peter spoke to the crowd about King David, reminding them that David had died and his body was still in the grave, but David died with a hope. Being a prophet, and knowing that God had promised Him that one of his descendants would sit upon the throne of Israel, David prophesied about Jesus' resurrection when he said: "That his soul was not left in hell, neither his flesh did see corruption" *(Acts 2:31)*.

Peter then proclaims, "This Jesus hath God raised up, whereof we all are witnesses" (*Acts 2:32*). Who were the witnesses? It could have been just the 12 Apostles, or it could have been all of the 120 who were present when the Holy Spirit was poured out. They were all eyewitnesses that this Jesus, who was crucified, had risen from the dead and now is exalted at the right hand of God. Peter continued by saying, what you are witnessing now is a fulfillment of the promise that the Father made from the beginning of time; this is the Promise of the Holy Ghost. The promise was made to Adam and Eve, to Abraham, to David, and now (*what you are hearing [tongues] and seeing [worship]*) the fulfillment of this prophecy had come to pass.

Peter climaxed his message with a statement (*Acts 2:36*) that all

Israel should know of a surety that God Himself has made this Jesus, who you crucified, both Lord (*Master*) and Christ (*the Messiah*). The words must have astonished the crowd. What Peter revealed to the multitude that day was that Jesus was their long-awaited Messiah. He had come from heaven to walk among them. He had come to visit with His people. Jesus would have set up His Kingdom then, if the people would have accepted Him, but they rejected Him, they crucified the one who was their only hope. Now what were they to do?

That was the question they asked Peter and the rest of the brethren. When they realized, what Peter had said to them, they didn't know what to do. The One whom Moses and the prophets promised them had come. He was to be their Savior, their Redeemer, their hope, but they put Him to death. So now they responded by saying, "Men and brethren, what shall we do" *(Acts 2:37)?* Tony Merida writes in the Christ-Centered Exposition, The Book of Acts:

> *The audience felt convicted because they were guilty. They were pierced because they realized they were the objects of God's wrath. They longed to be free from condemnation. Notice that they don't wait for Peter to offer an invitation. They ask him how they should respond to his message.* [3]

This message of hope and conviction pricked their hearts. They decided right then and there that they would respond to the call of the Gospel message.

The Only Response to the Preaching of the Gospel

What follows is Peter's answer to those who would be saved:

> *Then Peter said unto them, Repent, and be baptized every one of you in the name of Jesus Christ for the remission of sins, and ye shall receive the gift of the Holy Ghost. For the promise is unto you, and to your children, and to all that are afar off, even as many as the Lord our God shall call. (Acts 2:38-39)*

Acts 2:38 is the New Testament message of salvation. This is what it means to be Born Again of the Water and the Spirit *(John 3:3-5)*. You will see this mentioned both in exact and in similar ways throughout the Book of Acts.

Isn't it interesting that Peter did not tell the crowd to "Just believe on the Lord Jesus Christ," or to "recite the sinner's prayer," or to simply, "Accept the Lord as your personal savior?" I've heard and read these statements often as a response given to someone seeking salvation. For instance, I read this in a magazine: "Following Jesus Christ, No Matter the Cost."

> *Following Jesus means that you'll face trials and suffering, but it is worth it! Jesus taught that you must be born again. That can happen today if you will repent of your sin and by faith receive Christ as your Lord and Savior. If you've never done that, do so today ----- right here and now. If you will do that, God promises to give you a new beginning and a new life that is both abundant and eternal. Right now, wherever you are, you can begin a relationship with God. It's the most important thing you'll ever do.* [4]

Now I'm sure that this was written sincerely. I'm not mocking the writer or the article. It was a good article. Even the prayer could be viewed as a type of repentance. However, what I quoted is what people are generally told to do to seek God for salvation. But is this what the Apostles told people to do? In the Book of Acts when Jews, Gentiles, and even the Samaritans sought salvation through the preaching of the Word, the essence of Acts 2:38 is the usual answer, and this will be seen as we continue through this book.

You may wonder, why did Peter use these exact words? Did the Holy Ghost just inspire him at that moment? Had someone taught him what to say? Not only did someone give him these words to say, but it was given to him by Jesus Himself! Peter was given the keys to the kingdom *(Matthew 16:17-19)*, and it was revealed what to tell the Jews and then the Gentiles about how they must be saved and how to enter the Kingdom of God!

When did Jesus give Peter the words to say? The answer is found in the Great Commission. Most of the time when the Great Commission is discussed, we usually turn to the Book of Matthew to find out what Jesus said. However, all four Gospels have a part of this Great Commission, given as instruction after Jesus was risen and before His ascension. Notice how the following scriptures all relate to what Peter told the crowd when they asked him, "What shall we do?"

The preaching of the gospel should require a response. If one has faith to believe that Jesus died for our sins and rose again from the dead and is baptized, that one shall be saved. Faith and baptism are mentioned as part of the Great Commission in Mark.

And he said unto them, Go ye into all the world, and preach the gospel to every creature. He that believeth (has saving faith) and is baptized shall be saved; but he that believeth not shall be damned. And these signs shall follow them that believe; In my name shall they cast out devils; they shall speak with new tongues; (Mark 16:15-17)

In Matthew, Jesus tells us that we should go and teach His saving gospel to all the world. He tells them to baptize in the *name*. Father, Son and Holy Ghost are not names, they are titles, and these three titles all speak of Jesus.

Go ye therefore, and teach all nations, baptizing them in the name of the Father, and of the Son, and of the Holy Ghost: Teaching them to observe all things whatsoever I have commanded you: and, lo, I am with you alway, even unto the end of the world. Amen. (Matthew 28:19-20)

Jesus said, "I am come in my Father's name, and ye receive me not" (John 5:43). His Father's name is "Yahweh or Jehovah." Jesus' name is a compound name: "Yahweh Savior." This is very much like some of the compound names God used in the Old Testament to progressively reveal Himself to His people, such as "Yahweh-Jireh" (*The Lord will provide*) or "Yahweh-Shalom" (*The Lord our Peace*). When the fulness of time had come, God revealed Himself by the Name above all other names: Jesus (*The Lord our Savior*).

We know that His name is Jesus because that was the name the angel told Joseph to name him (*Matthew 1:21*). What about the Holy Spirit? Does He have a name? Jesus told His disciples speaking of the Holy Spirit:

> *Even the Spirit of truth; whom the world cannot receive, because it seeth him not, neither knoweth him: but ye know him; for he dwelleth with you and shall be in you. (John 14:17)*

Jesus told His disciples that He would be with them always (*Matthew 28:20*). How would He be with them? In Spirit, within them! Paul wrote to the Gentiles saying:

> *To whom God would make known what is the riches of the glory of this mystery among the Gentiles; which is Christ in you, the hope of glory: (Colossians 1:27)*

And Jesus said: "But the Comforter, which is the Holy Ghost, whom the Father will send in my name, he shall teach you all things, and bring all things to your remembrance, whatsoever I have said unto you" (*John 14:26*). So, the titles in Matthew 28:19 all point to Jesus and that is why when Peter spoke in Acts Chapter 2, he said to baptize in the Name of Jesus Christ.

Continuing on with the Great Commission, the command to baptize in the Name of Jesus is even more defined in Luke:

> *And said unto them, Thus it is written, and thus it behoved Christ to suffer, and to rise from the dead the third day: And that repentance and remission of sins should be preached in his name among all nations, beginning at Jerusalem. And ye are witnesses of these things. And, behold, I send the promise of my Father upon you: but tarry ye in the city of Jerusalem, until ye be endued with power from on high. (Luke 24:46-49)*

In Luke, Jesus tells us that there must be repentance (*turning away from sin*) and that remission of sins should be preached in *His name*. In Acts 2:38, Peter mentions that baptism is for the remission of sins. So, baptism must be in the Name of Jesus, not merely the titles of Father, Son, Holy Ghost. Why? Because Jesus is the only name given to men for salvation according to Acts 4:12: "Neither is there salvation in any other: for there is none other name under heaven given among men, whereby we must be saved" *(Acts 4:12)*. Ben Witherington connects baptism in Jesus name with calling on the Lord in his commentary on Acts:

> *The two parts of the speech material in vv. 14-40 have a certain unity and coherence: (1) 'to call upon the name of the Lord' (v. 21) is another way of speaking about the event that involves being baptized 'in the name of Jesus Christ' (v. 38)* [5]

When we examine the baptism of the Apostle Paul, we see that is the case:

> *And now why tarriest thou? arise, and be baptized, and wash away thy sins, calling on the name of the Lord. (Acts 22:16)*

Some people remark that they would rather obey Jesus than Peter, but let's examine this. Isn't all scripture written by inspiration of God? (*2 Timothy 3:16*) Isn't all scripture profitable for doctrine, reproof, correction, and for instruction in righteousness? There is no contradiction in the Scripture. Also, wasn't Matthew one of the disciples who was in the upper room when the Holy Ghost fell on them? Wasn't he also present when Peter told the crowd these words? Why didn't Matthew object and tell Peter he was incorrect? Interesting, isn't it?

So right now, we see in the Great Commission that Jesus told us we need to have Faith, Repentance, and Baptism in His Name for remission of sins. We have looked at Jesus' words of the Great Commission in Matthew, Mark and Luke. Now let's look in John's gospel account of the Great Commission:

> *Then the same day at evening, being the first day of the week, when the doors were shut where the disciples were assembled for fear of the Jews, came Jesus and stood in the midst, and saith unto them, Peace be unto you. And when he had so said, he shewed unto them his hands and his side. Then were the disciples glad, when they saw the Lord. Then said Jesus to them again, Peace be unto you: as my Father hath sent me, even so send I you. And when he had said this, he breathed on them, and saith unto them, Receive ye the Holy Ghost: Whose soever sins ye remit, they are remitted unto them; and whose soever sins ye retain, they are retained. (John 20:19-23)*

Jesus showed up after His resurrection in a place where the disciples were assembled. In verse 22, the scripture says that Jesus breathed on them and said, "Receive ye the Holy Ghost." Many believe that Jesus gave the Holy Ghost to the disciples at that time, but did He? If so, then why did Jesus tell all the disciples that they were to go and wait for the promise of the Father? Jesus said that He had to go away, that is, ascend back to heaven before the Holy Ghost could come (*John 16:7*). Ten days later they were all filled with the Holy Ghost with evidence of speaking in tongues.

There was also someone missing that night when Jesus appeared to the disciples; Thomas was not among them. Why would Jesus have given the Holy Ghost that night when one of His disciples was not present? Could it be that Jesus gave them a foreshadowing that night how they would receive the Holy Ghost? This is what is inferred. So, we see in the Great Commission of all the Gospels that Jesus told His disciples exactly what to tell those who responded to the gospel message in faith. Faith, Repentance, Baptism in His Name for remission of sins and receiving the gift of the Holy Ghost.

If we compare the gospels' accounts with Acts 2:38, there is only one response we should give when people respond to the gospel by asking, "What shall we do?" Ben Witherington replies in his commentary on Acts about Acts 2:38:

> *What one can say is that Luke intends his audience to know that repentance, faith, baptism, the name of Jesus, and reception of the Spirit were all important elements when the matter of 'what must we do' or how people enter the community of Christ comes up.* [6]

He continues by saying:

> *It is thus quite correct to stress that in Acts 2 we see repentance (and faith) leading to baptism, the forgiveness of sins, and the reception of the Holy Spirit. This was apparently normally the case. Acts then provides us with a record of 'missionary' baptisms, stories about the conversion of those on the outside who are then brought into the family of Christian faith.* [6]

What Does the Bible Say About the Phrase "Faith Alone?"

Before someone can be saved, they must have faith. However, there is an incorrect teaching that says salvation is based on "faith alone." By using that phrase, scholars and commentators will teach that solely by believing in your heart by faith you are saved. This they do because they teach that to be baptized and to seek the Holy Ghost is to teach a salvation by works. The Bible says that: **"For by grace are ye saved through faith; and that not of yourselves: it is the gift of God: Not of works, lest any man should boast"** *(Ephesians 2:8-9).*

Now I believe that we are saved by our faith. Without faith it is impossible to receive anything from God (*Hebrews 11:6*). It is by faith that we receive God's grace that saves us. However, in keeping with the whole of scripture there must be a response or an action to the gospel when it is preached to show our faith which is what James is writing about in his epistle: "Ye see then how that by works a man is justified, and not by faith only" *(James 2:24).* The NIV Application Commentary on the Book of Acts says this about a response to the gospel:

"The Ethiopian eunuch realized that he needed to respond to Philip's message. Thus, when they came to some water, he suggested baptism (v. 36). We are not told how Philip brought him to this point, but here, as in all the evangelistic situations in Acts, a response is implied. Similarly, in all our witness we must have in mind the goal of a response to the gospel. This is not popular in our pluralistic society. People have accepted dialogue as a suitable way to discuss religion. But the end of such dialogue is a mutual enrichment. The evangelism of Acts, by contrast, always aims at a response." [7]

As another example, let's look at the Patriarch Abraham and what Paul says of him in Romans Chapter 4:

For if Abraham were justified by works, he hath whereof to glory; but not before God. For what saith the scripture? Abraham believed God, and it was counted unto him for righteousness. Now to him that worketh is the reward not reckoned of grace, but of debt. (Romans 4:2-4)

Abraham's faith in God is what affected his justification. It was through his action to sacrifice Isaac that God saw his faith (of course God already knew it). He was willing to sacrifice Isaac because he believed that God could raise him from the dead to keep His promise to him. After the Lord stopped Abraham from sacrificing Isaac, this is what He told him:

And he said, Lay not thine hand upon the lad, neither do thou any thing unto him: for now I know that thou fearest God, seeing thou hast not withheld thy son, thine only son from me. (Genesis 22:12)

Notice what God said to Abraham, "Now I know that thou fearest God, seeing thou hast not withheld thy son, thine only son from me." Again, his action was a response of his faith. Therefore, when we repent, are baptized in Jesus' name, and receive the Holy Ghost, we are acting in faith by being obedient to the command that Jesus gave His Apostles to preach. That is the response to the gospel.

I find as I read many commentaries that scholars say we are saved by "faith alone." This always used to annoy me because I couldn't find that wording in the KJV version of the Bible. I thought that there must be other versions that use that terminology. Recently, I did a search through most of the more popular Bible translations (*AMP, NKJV, NCV, NET, ASV*), and to my surprise not one of these translations use the term "faith alone" to teach that it is by "faith alone" we are saved.

As I searched through these translations (*NLT, ESV, NASB, NIV, CJB, RSV*), the wording "faith alone" appeared only one time and that was in reference to James 2:24 which states: "Ye see then how that by works a man is justified, and not by faith only" *(James 2:24).*

"What are you saying, Joe?" you may ask. "Are you saying we're saved by works?"

In short, no. I have faith in the saving work of Jesus Christ. I believe that He died for me, was buried, and has risen from the dead. I believe that by faith I am saved because, and only because, of the grace of God. If God had not extended grace to us, we could believe all we want to; we could repent and be dunked in water all day long and it would profit us nothing. The act of baptism wouldn't save us. It is when, as Brian Kinsey states in his book, *Ephesians, A Commentary, The Brides Pearl:*

> *God has given everyone a measure of faith (Romans 12:3), but each person must deposit that faith in Christ to receive the benefits of God's grace. Once faith is put in Christ, Jesus releases His grace, and His grace releases the resurrection power that changes the life of the believer (Titus 3:5).* [8]

In the article, "Cheap Grace," found in the Pentecostal Life Magazine, Feb. 2022 issue, written by Scott Graham, it provides another thought-proving response to the importance of faith, grace, and obedience:

Yes, we respond in faith and that faith is demonstrated by obedience, but without God's grace, all our acts of obedience would be nothing but vain practices devoid of any spiritual consequence. [9]

Graham continues by saying:

When the love of God reaches for us to tug our heart toward Him, that's grace. When His Word brings us to repentance so our sins might be forgiven, that's grace. When our sinful past is purged so we might enjoy new life, that's grace. When the Spirit of God guides our lives thereafter in paths that please Him, and that are spiritually healthy for us, that's grace. [9]

So, unless God extends His grace to us, it doesn't matter what we do, we could never be saved. In fact, when you examine what Paul said in both Romans and Galatians about works, we find that he was talking to Judiazers telling them that we are saved by faith and not the "works of the law." When Paul was referring to works, he was speaking about returning to the works of the law for their salvation.

Where is boasting then? It is excluded. By what law? of works? Nay: but by the law of faith. Therefore we conclude that a man is justified by faith without the deeds of the law. (Romans 3:27-28)

Knowing that a man is not justified by the works of the law, but by the faith of Jesus Christ, even we have believed in Jesus Christ, that we might be justified by the faith of Christ, and not by the works of the law: for by the works of the law shall no flesh be justified. (Galatians 2:16)

Paul was stressing the fact that New Testament believers are saved by grace through faith. But Paul never used the term "faith alone." I wonder why so many preachers, teachers, writers, and others insist on using this wording "faith alone," when that phrase doesn't appear in the Bible? When we search the scriptures, especially in the Great

Commission, we see that Jesus told the Apostles exactly what the people had to do in order to be saved.

Final Thoughts

In verse 39 of Acts 2, Peter said that "the promise is unto you (Jews), and to your children, and to all that are afar off (*Samaritans and Gentiles*), even as many as the Lord our God *shall call*." So, everyone who calls on the Name of the Lord, and all those who believe they are the called of the Lord Jesus, should then repent, be baptized in the name of Jesus Christ, and should receive the gift of the Holy Ghost, evidenced by speaking in unknown tongues as the Spirit gives the utterance, just like the disciples did on that first Pentecost Sunday.

And with many other words did he testify and exhort, saying, Save yourselves from this untoward generation. Then they that gladly received his word were baptized: and the same day there were added unto them about three thousand souls. (Acts 2:40-41)

Peter continued preaching his message, instructing the crowd by other words, most likely ministering through the Holy Ghost, and testifying about and exalting the Lord Jesus Christ. He told the people to "Save themselves from this untoward generation." The word "untoward" means "crooked, perverse, or froward." How could they save themselves? The answer is by obeying the word which was preached that day. They had to decide to either obey the words that Peter preached or else to walk away and not take advantage of God's glorious gift of life!

Peter had preached his sermon offering the people the way of salvation and their entrance into the Kingdom of God. About 3,000 souls answered the call of God that morning. What a great outpouring of the Holy Ghost! However, you have to wonder that if 3,000 souls were saved that morning, how many people were present to hear these words of eternal life but walked away unmoved by the message? The scripture doesn't tell us how many unbelievers, mockers, skeptics, and doubters were present to hear that first Gospel message.

Unfortunately, wherever the Gospel is preached, there may be those who will resist the Word of God. Scripture seems to indicate in the New Testament that as the Gospel goes forth, there will be believers and unbelievers. Jesus died for all mankind, no matter the ethnicity, nationality, or religion, but only those who will receive the message of the Gospel and obey the call of God, will be saved and will enter into the Kingdom of God.

5
THEY CONTINUED

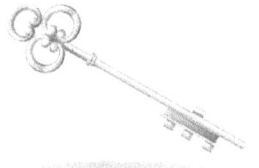

Follow-through. According to the dictionary, it means "the continuing of a task or action to its conclusion." There's an old adage that reminds us that it's not only about starting, but it is the finishing that is most important. Throughout my many years in church, I realized that follow-through is often difficult to achieve, but in the kingdom, it is required.

I have seen many good programs and ideas, only to find in a few years, everything fell apart. I heard of crusades used to start churches. These areas are usually canvased by sending out flyers, putting advertisements in local papers, and by just meeting people in the streets and giving them an invitation to attend a Pentecostal Crusade. Some come and believe through the preaching of the Word of God. They start out with great expectations walking by faith only to fall away during the days, months, or even years to come. Many good contacts are made. A man with a burden for the area where the crusade was held is installed as a Pastor. The Church starts out with great momentum, but after only a short time, all hopes are dashed and all good intentions fall far short of the goal.

Why is this? The intense energy, the money spent, the passions that were once so strong, have dissipated. There are probably many reasons why these things happen. They happen in business, in life experience, and in Church ministry. They all started well, but they didn't continue! There was no follow-through.

> *And they continued stedfastly in the apostles' doctrine and fellowship, and in breaking of bread, and in prayers. And fear came upon every soul: and many wonders and signs were done by the apostles. And all that believed were together, and had all things common; And sold their possessions and goods, and parted them to all men, as every man had need. And they, continuing daily with one accord in the temple, and breaking bread from house to house, did eat their meat with gladness and singleness of heart, Praising God, and having favour with all the people. And the Lord added to the church daily such as should be saved. (Acts 2:42-47)*

The Day of Pentecost was one of those times when things started out on a big note. The Holy Ghost fell on 120 people in the upper room. Peter preached to the crowd telling them that they crucified their Messiah and many of the people responded, "Men and brethren, what shall we do?" Peter then tells them exactly what Jesus instructed him to tell people as said in the Great Commission. His answer to them was:

> *Then Peter said unto them, Repent, and be baptized every one of you in the name of Jesus Christ for the remission of sins, and ye shall receive the gift of the Holy Ghost. For the promise is unto you, and to your children, and to all that are afar off, even as many as the Lord our God shall call. (Acts 2:38-39)*

Following Peter's answer, 3000 souls were baptized in the only name given among men whereby we must be saved: Jesus (*Acts 4:12*). I can hardly think of a greater example of something that started with a bang. However, how did the Apostles keep the energy level high enough and keep the passions flowing so that this great moment didn't fall apart? The answer is, "They continued steadfastly!" The Greek word for "steadfastly" means to be "constantly diligent." This means that there was a great desire in the heart of those new Christians to continually hear the Word of God preached and to learn more of what Jesus instructed these twelve men who were the closest to the Lord. They were faithful in keeping the Lord's Supper and in fellowship with the other believers. Prayer meetings in houses and in the temple were a daily occurrence. This is how they stayed close to one another and how they survived the onslaught of persecution that came upon them.

We would do well in our day, considering that we are living in the last days, to be as diligent as the early church was in these areas. As we saw during the past couple of years, most of our churches were shut down due to the Covid-19 pandemic. Our government actually forced us to close our doors. At the same time, bars and liquor stores remained open for business. They were considered important while the spiritual well-being of our country was not. Winston Churchill once said, "Those that fail to learn from history are doomed to repeat it." I would never want to see this happen again, and it starts with going back to the basics.

We need to have a network of smaller groups where our church could meet in homes across our nation. Why? Because we lost so many people due to the pandemic that we should never let the government have the opportunity to be able to shut our churches down again. If we had smaller groups then we could at any moment go underground and keep the believers together.

Another solution is when a church congregation gets to a certain size, it should branch out and start a daughter work. We should adopt the "Walmart" formula for success. What does this mean? It means we should have a church every 15-20 miles away. Why? Because in this day, most people are not willing to travel far to go anywhere, but especially to church. We can never have too many churches! I was teaching a bible study to two women a few years ago and was encouraging them to come to our church services. When they heard that the church was

25 miles away, they said it was too far. People are very busy today and are not willing to drive far distances to attend church, when they don't realize the benefit that there is in a church that has a Spirit-filled congregation. They say, "There is a church a few blocks from where I live, why should I drive 25 miles to go where you go?" If there was a church 10-15 minutes away, would they come? Probably!

The New Testament saints met on a daily basis. That's why God could add unto the church *daily*. They didn't just have meetings on Sunday and midweek like we do today. Church was their life. I'm afraid that today church attendance is secondary to many Christians. Christianity is not the most important thing in many Christians lives.

Our small groups should also be trained in the ministry of discipleship. Bringing someone to church and praying with them to receive the Holy Ghost is great. But that is only the beginning of their new life in Christ. But we shouldn't stop there. That new convert needs to be discipled. It's not a matter of tallying great numbers coming into our churches that is important. It's not even important reporting that great numbers of people have been baptized as fantastic as that can be. We need to make sure that we do our best to train and disciple these new converts. We should want them to receive a true and lasting life change experience. That would take considerable one-on-one mentoring. This is what the first century New Testament Church did. Maybe we should learn from their successes. The scripture says that these first century Christians "continued steadfastly." What did they continue in? According to Scripture, they continued in 1.) Apostolic doctrine, 2.) Fellowship, 3.) Breaking of bread, and 4.) Prayer.

Apostolic Doctrine

The majority of the reason that the Early Church was successful was because they continued to be consistent in a few different areas of their new life in Christ. They continued in the Apostles' Doctrine *(Acts 2:42)*. People are usually good with coming to Church, or attending a home fellowship group, or care group. They don't usually mind singing, or praying for people's needs, or even enjoying fellowship supported by some food. However, just let the Pastor, or group leader, begin to read scripture and teach what the scriptures are saying, and all of a sudden, those same people, begin to get uneasy. They say that doctrine divides. Why do we have to talk about doctrine?

I guess the simple answer to this is that the word "doctrine" in scripture simply means "teaching." Everyone likes to hear preaching about love. All we need is love. Do we realize that "love" is a doctrine? How about the wonderful grace of God? Are we thankful for grace? Do we realize that "grace" is also a doctrine? So, if someone doesn't like doctrine, then they wouldn't have liked listening to Jesus when He taught the Sermon on the Mount. What about Jesus' teaching on forgiveness, pride, submission to authority, adultery, greed, along with a multitude of other sins? Without doctrine there is no foundation. Without a foundation, the house cannot stand.

> *Whosoever cometh to me, and heareth my sayings, and doeth them, I will shew you to whom he is like: He is like a man which built an house, and digged deep, and laid the foundation on a rock: and when the flood arose, the stream beat vehemently upon that house, and could not shake it: for it was founded upon a rock. But he that heareth, and doeth not, is like a man that without a foundation built an house upon the earth; against which the stream did beat vehemently, and immediately it fell; and the ruin of that house was great. (Luke 6:47-49)*

While it may be true that doctrine divides, this may not necessarily be a bad thing. Doctrine does divide! It divides good from evil, light from darkness, truth from error. The Apostle Paul concurs with this thought:

> *Don't team up with those who are unbelievers. How can righteousness be a partner with wickedness? How can light live with darkness? What harmony can there be between Christ and the devil? How can a believer be*

a partner with an unbeliever? And what union can there be between God's temple and idols? (2 Corinthians 6:14-16 NLT)

The Apostles' Doctrine is what kept the early church on the right track. Much of the doctrine of the early church was based upon what the disciples learned from Jesus, from the Old Testament Scriptures and from any true New Testament teachings that were circulating (2 Peter3:15-16). Without the truth of God's Word, the early church would not have made it past the 1st Century due to false teachers bringing in all kind of damnable heresies.

But there were false prophets also among the people, even as there shall be false teachers among you, who privily shall bring in damnable heresies, even denying the Lord that bought them, and bring upon themselves swift destruction. (2 Peter 2:1)

And it is no difference today. Jesus warned us that there would be false teachers that would come in the last days and claim to be the Messiah.

For there shall arise false Christs, and false prophets, and shall shew great signs and wonders; insomuch that, if it were possible, they shall deceive the very elect. (Matthew 24:24)

Beware of false prophets, which come to you in sheep's clothing, but inwardly they are ravening wolves. (Matthew 7:15)

The Apostle Paul also admonished us:

For such are false apostles, deceitful workers, transforming themselves into the apostles of Christ. (2 Corinthians 11:13)

The Apostle John also spoke of this in his epistle:

> *Beloved, believe not every spirit, but try the spirits whether they are of God: because many false prophets are gone out into the world. (1 John 4:1)*

In the last days one will rise along with the Antichrist to deceive the whole world. This one is known as the False Prophet. Jesus spoke of that day to be a day of great deception, and that, unless the days were shortened, not even the elect would be saved (*Matthew 24:22*). Without sound doctrine, we would be swept away with all the deception, lies, and the wiles of the devil. The Apostles' teaching would have been very important because Jesus promised that the Holy Ghost would guide them into all truth and it would teach them things to come.

> *Howbeit when he, the Spirit of truth, is come, he will guide you into all truth: for he shall not speak of himself; but whatsoever he shall hear, that shall he speak: and he will shew you things to come. (John 16:13)*

In the process of time, the church developed a full and complete body of teaching, so that when Paul met with the Ephesian elders for the last time, he declared that he was "pure from the blood of all men," because he didn't shrink from declaring to all men the whole counsel of God. As stated in the Story of God Bible commentary:

> *The apostles teaching it's not only based on what Jesus communicated to them personally, but it also follows the model of Jesus' teaching that turns to the Scripture to discover what 'Moses and all the Prophets' say about Christ.* [1]

Fellowship

The early Church also continued in fellowship. The Greek word for fellowship in Acts 2:42 is "koinonia" which means "to share in," "participation," "communion." Fellowship is more than just getting together or hanging out with someone. Fellowship is the mutual benefit we receive when we share our life experiences with others. Fellowship is:

> *That common life of close brotherhood in which all that they did was done in common, and all that they possessed was possessed in common (this was done voluntarily, not by compulsion), so that there seemed to be but one heart and one mind.* [2]

In fact, this is exactly what the early Church did. The Preachers Outline and Sermon Bible states:

> *The Holy Spirit creates a spiritual union by melting and molding the heart of the Christian believer to the hearts of other believers. He attaches the life of one believer to the lives of other believers. Through the spirit of God, believers become one in life and purpose. They have a joint life sharing their blessings and needs and gifts together.* [3]

The concept of fellowship among the believers is prevalent in Scripture:

> *Just as our bodies have many parts and each part has a special function, so it is with Christ's body. We are many parts of one body, and we all belong to each other. (Romans NLT 12:4-5)*

> *But if we are living in the light, as God is in the light, then we have fellowship with each other, and the blood of Jesus, his Son, cleanses us from all sin. (1 John 1:7)*

> *And let us not neglect our meeting together, as some people do, but encourage one another, especially now that the day of his return is drawing near. (Hebrews NLT 10:25)*

> *And all that believed were together and had all things common; And sold their possessions and goods, and parted them to all men, as every man had need. (Acts 2:44-45)*

This was not something that was forced upon them to do, but it was probably done more out of necessity and out of love for the brethren. Those who had more gave to those who had less. Fellowship, which is the Greek word "koinonia," is spoken of in different ways throughout the New Testament. In Romans 15:26 the word is used as "contribution."

> *For it hath pleased them of Macedonia and Achaia to make a certain contribution for the poor saints which are at Jerusalem. (Romans 15:26)*

It was the saints in Macedonia and Achaia who had a desire to share what blessings God had given to them with the poor saints in Jerusalem, who were most likely enduring suffering and persecution. And isn't that the way it should be? We, whom God has blessed, should in turn bless those that are in need. The scripture is, without doubt, very clear on this matter.

> *But whoso hath this world's good, and seeth his brother have need, and shutteth up his bowels of compassion from him, how dwelleth the love of God in him? (1 John 3:17)*

How can we love our brothers and sisters and yet stand by and not help them when they have need, especially if God has abundantly blessed us? In fact, that may well be the reason why God has so blessed us. Therefore, we would be negligent if we did not share our blessings.

The same Greek word for "koinonia" was also translated as "distribution" in 2 Corinthians 9:13-14, as the Apostle Paul praised the Corinthian Church for caring for those in need.

> *Whiles by the experiment of this ministration they glorify God for your professed subjection unto the gospel of Christ, and for your liberal distribution unto them, and unto all men; And by their prayer for you, which long after you for the exceeding grace of God in you.* (*2 Corinthians 9:13-14*)

The liberal giving of their gifts to the brethren in Jerusalem proved their obedience to the Gospel, and the saints in Jerusalem prayed for the overflowing grace God had given to the Corinthians.

We also see the same Greek word translated as "communion" as in the Lord's Supper.

> *The cup of blessing which we bless, is it not the communion of the blood of Christ? The bread which we break, is it not the communion of the body of Christ?* (*1 Corinthians 10:16*)

The Lord's Supper is one of the greatest fellowships to have, committing ourselves to Christ, surrounded by like-minded believers. William Burkett concurs:

> *That one great end and design of Christ in the institution of his supper was this, that believers might enjoy a sweet fellowship and communion with himself therein.* [4]

These examples show the importance of fellowship among believers and with the Lord. Through our Christian Fellowship we can encourage and strengthen one another as we walk together in truth. This will be especially true as we draw nearer to the 2nd coming of Jesus Christ.

> *But if we walk in the light, as he is in the light, we have fellowship one with another, and the blood of Jesus Christ his Son cleanseth us from all sin.* (*1 John 1:7*)

Breaking of Bread

Part of fellowship involves the *breaking of bread*. There are differences of opinion on what the term *breaking of bread* actually means. For some, this is speaking of communion or the Lord's Supper. Others believe that it has more to do with the saints meeting together in someone's home for a meal. This could also be what is referred to in Jude as "feasts of charity" or "love feasts." This seems to have been the practice of the early Church. As Stanley Horton writes in his commentary:

> *The breaking of bread some writers take to mean not only the Lord's supper, but it also includes table fellowship. Believers could not observe the Lord's supper in the temple, so this was done in their homes, at first in connection with a meal (since Jesus instituted it at the close of the Passover meal).* [5]

Make no mistake. The breaking of bread, both as participation in fellowship and in communion, is mentioned in Scripture. As explained in Mounce's Expository Dictionary:

> *In the New Testament it always occurs in reference to bread. In the first century, the common practice was to break bread with one's hand rather than slicing it with a knife. Jesus broke the bread to feed the multitude (Matthew 14:19). Paul broke bread on the boat as he headed for Rome (Acts 27:35). Early Christians often had meals together, expressed by breaking bread.* [6]

After Jesus' resurrection, He walked with two disciples on the way to Emmaus. Though the disciples didn't recognize Him physically, the words He spoke burned in their hearts. So, they decided to have this stranger come in for the night. As they sat to eat, this is what happened.

And it came to pass, as he sat at meat with them, he took bread, and blessed it, and brake, and gave to them. And their eyes were opened, and they knew him; and he vanished out of their sight. (Luke 24:30)

Not only does breaking of bread seek fellowship among believers, but it also refers to sharing in communion. Life Application Bible on 1 Corinthians 11:20-21 explains: "Breaking of Bread refers to Communion Services that were celebrated in remembrance of Jesus... patterned after the Last Supper that Jesus had held with His disciples before His death." [7]

It is not clear that this was a type of the Lord's Supper. Usually, the host would be the one to break the bread, which was common for all meals. Jesus did this at the Last Supper meal before instituting the New Covenant in His blood. Though He broke the bread here, there is no mention of the cup of wine because Jesus disappeared out of their sight. Yet, the Apostle Paul taught us about the Last Supper in 1 Corinthians Chapter 11: "For as often as ye eat this bread, and drink this cup, ye do shew the Lord's death till he come" *(1 Corinthians 11:26)*.

What do these examples show us? First, the word "shew" in 1 Corinthians 11 means "to declare, preach, speak of, teach." When we share in the Last Supper, through communion, we are declaring, preaching, and teaching that the Lord Jesus Christ died for our sins, and we now are all awaiting, anxiously looking for His Second Coming in the clouds of glory. That's not all. The examples show us that we don't have to wait for church communion to break bread with fellow believers. All of this is about fellowship and continuing in the faith...together.

Prayer

Although mentioned as the last of the four, it certainly is not last in importance. Actually, it is more likely that prayer is most important. The simplest definition of prayer is: Talking to God or communing with God. A better definition might be that prayer is an intense longing, desire, or need expressed in words to God as we communicate these longings of our deepest feelings to Him.

Prayer is a dialogue (not a monologue). This means we talk to God, and God talks to us. It is in prayer that you are nearer to God than at any other time. Our prayers can have a great purpose because the Bible tells us that God responds to prayer when we pray in faith! (*Matthew 21:22*)

What does the Bible say about prayer of the saints? The scripture is full of examples of prayer.

- Prayer was a daily spiritual exercise for the Apostles (*Acts 3:1*);
- The Apostles continually gave themselves to prayer (*Acts 6:4*);
- Prayer delivered Peter out of prison (*Acts 12:5*).
- James tells us that the effectual fervent *prayer* of a righteous man availeth much (*James 5:16*).
- Jesus told us to pray for those who persecute you (*Matthew 5:44*).
- Pray that we don't fall into temptation; pray for the things you desire (*Mark 11:24*);
- Pray that the Lord of the Harvest would send laborers into the field (*Luke 10:2*);
- Pray for one another (*1 Thessalonians 5:25*; *James 5:16*) and
- Pray without ceasing (*1 Thessalonians ` 5:17*).

In the Gospels we read of the hours Jesus spent in prayer, sometimes all night in communion with the Father. These facts testify to the absolute importance of prayer in the Christian's life. Prayer is the greatest privilege which God has given to the saints, but unfortunately, it is the one thing many Christians neglect.

A leading denomination conducted a survey to see how much time its ministers, pastors, and leaders spent in prayer daily. The average time was 7 minutes. If that is all the time that we have to give to God in our day, then I'm afraid we may not see the victories we desire to see. And when we consider that when we are in prayer, we are closer to God then at any other time, why wouldn't we spend more time in prayer?

Prayer is necessary for our spiritual survival. Prayer adds the anointing to our singing, preaching, teaching, witnessing. We can do nothing good for God or anyone else without prayer. Without prayer we will never have victory in this life. When we consider these things, it is a wonder why prayer is not that important to many Christians today.

The Apostles' Results

From these verses in Acts 2:42-47, it would seem like the Christians lived together in unity, spending much of their day between worshipping in the Temple and sharing meals together in people's homes.

And they, continuing daily with one accord in the temple, and breaking bread from house to house, did eat their meat with gladness and singleness of heart. (Acts 2:46)

It seems, at least in the beginning, that community life was closely intertwined. Their lives seemed to be so simple and yet it was very powerful. Miracles and wonders were done by the Apostles (*Acts 2:43*). This was a continuation of Jesus' ministry; God was now working through the believers, specifically through the Apostles. Jesus told His disciples that they would do even greater works than He did.

Verily, verily, I say unto you, He that believeth on me, the works that I do shall he do also; and greater works than these shall he do; because I go unto my Father. (John 14:12)

There are two instances in Acts where miracles were performed in very different ways than how Jesus performed them. In one instance just Peter's shadow would fall upon the sick and they would be healed:

> *Insomuch that they brought forth the sick into the streets, and laid them on beds and couches, that at the least the shadow of Peter passing by might overshadow some of them. (Acts 5:15)*

They would also bring handkerchiefs to the apostles to pray over them. When these cloths were placed upon the sick, they were healed. It was never recorded in the scriptures that Jesus ever healed in this manner. These miracles were never meant to be just an outward display of power, but they were to be signs following the believers and confirming the word of God that had been preached. I believe this is how it should be today. Miracles and healings should follow the preached word. We should expect to see God do wonders in the earth like he did for the First Century Church.

Final Thoughts

What would have happened if Jesus's disciples never acted on His commands? What if the disciples were too scared? What if they became too busy? Would this great message of salvation have been lost forever and all of mankind doomed to an eternity without the Lord? But they did act, and thankfully they continued steadfastly in the work of the Lord.

These early Christians continued daily in unity in the Temple and sharing meals from house to house. They ate their meals with gladness (*joy, rejoicing*) and singleness of heart, which could mean "purity of purpose." As the Christ-Centered Exposition Commentary stated:

> *The Church lived out this shared life "every day." They were involved in one another's lives. While the church has to love those outside the family in order to fulfill its mission, a healthy church meets together as a family regularly.* [8]

They were praising God and had favor with all the people. And the result of their continuing to live and preach the Gospel was: *"...And the Lord added to the church daily such as should be saved." (Acts 2:47)* The New American Commentary says this about the last verses of Acts 2:

> *Verses 42-46 give an ideal portrait of the young Christian community, witnessing the Spirit's presence in the miracles of the apostles, sharing their possessions with the needy among them, sharing their witness in the temple, sharing themselves in the intimacy of their table fellowship. Their common life was marked by praise of God, joy in the faith, and sincerity of heart. And in it all they experienced the favor of the nonbelievers and continual blessings of God-given growth.* [9]

The young New Testament Church continued in the doctrine, fellowship, breaking of bread, and in prayers, and this is what fueled their passion and gave them the spiritual power to carry on the work that Jesus started. We have this Gospel message today because the early church continued to live and preach the Gospel.

Now it's our turn! Once we receive the revelation of truth and submit ourselves to the truth of the Word, we must continue in the faith. What does this mean? We must also continue to live passionate lives for Jesus Christ and to continue to preach this One True Gospel so that we can pass it on to the next generation! They continued; so, must we!

6

BEFORE THE JEWISH COUNCIL

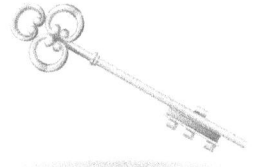

It was May of 2006. My wife and I were sitting in our car, and we were feeling quite anxious. We had just moved to South Carolina in November of 2005, and we didn't know many people except for our Pastor and his wife and another two friends. I had just applied for my local minister's license. We were waiting to be called before the district board as was the custom for new ministers, and we didn't know what to expect. We had only heard rumors of what it would be like. We would be asked questions by the ministers of the district board as they scrutinized our answers, and we would have to define the expected goals of our ministry. The board would review my application and ask questions about anything that wasn't clear to them, maybe even personal things about our lives. As it turned out, our anxiety was turned to peace. The district board gladly excepted us into their fellowship, and we left feeling very relieved.

After the healing of the lame man in Acts 3, the Jewish leaders brought Peter and John before them commanding them never to speak in the name of Jesus again. I can only imagine how difficult this must have been for them. What would the leaders do if the Apostles disobeyed them? Were they as nervous as I was waiting to go before the district board? No, they didn't seem to be. Filled with the power of the Holy Ghost, Peter and John appeared before the Jewish council and boldly told them that they must obey God rather than men. Then they continued to proclaim the Gospel of the Lord Jesus Christ.

Let's be clear: the Jewish leadership of that time period did not approve of the disciples' actions. They probably assumed the death of Jesus would end these "signs and wonders." But that is not what happened. "And fear came upon every soul: and many wonders and signs were done by the apostles" (*Acts 2:43*). The apostles soon found out that they would have to answer for these events, but as we'll discover throughout this chapter, they refused to be deterred from what Christ had called them to do.

Signs and Wonders Lead to the Gospel Message

Now Peter and John went up together into the temple at the hour of prayer, being the ninth hour. And a certain man lame from his mother's womb was carried, whom they laid daily at the gate of the temple which is called Beautiful, to ask alms of them that entered into the temple; Who seeing Peter and John about to go into the temple asked an alms. And Peter, fastening his eyes upon him with John, said, Look on us. And he gave heed unto them, expecting to receive something of them. Then Peter said, Silver and gold have I none; but such as I have give I thee: In the name of Jesus Christ of Nazareth rise up and walk. And he took him by the right hand and lifted him up: and immediately his feet and ancle bones received strength. And he leaping up stood, and walked, and entered with them into the temple, walking, and leaping, and praising God. And all the people saw him walking and praising God: And they knew that it was he which sat for alms at the Beautiful gate of the temple: and they were filled with wonder and amazement at that which had happened unto him. And as the lame man which was healed held Peter and John, all the people ran together unto them in the porch that is called Solomon's, greatly wondering. And when Peter saw it, he answered unto the people, Ye men of Israel, why marvel ye at this? or why look ye so earnestly on us, as though by our own power or holiness we had made this man to walk? The God of Abraham, and of Isaac, and of Jacob, the God of our fathers, hath glorified his Son Jesus; whom ye delivered up, and denied him in the presence of Pilate, when he was determined to let him go. But ye denied the Holy One and the Just and desired a murderer to be granted unto you; And killed the Prince of life, whom God hath raised from the dead; whereof we are witnesses. (Acts 3:1-15)

As Chapter 3 opens, the Apostles Peter and John were going up to the temple to pray at the ninth hour (*3 p.m.*). On the way to the temple, they met a blind man who was sitting at the Temple Gate called Beautiful, and he was begging. This man was lame from his mother's womb, and he was carried to the temple every day to beg for money. Peter and John must have passed by this blind beggar many times on their way to pray. Something was different this day as they approached him. The man asked the Apostles for money. Instead of giving him money, Peter said that he had something else to give him, something much better than money.

Then Peter said, Silver and gold have I none; but such as I have give I thee: In the name of Jesus Christ of Nazareth rise up and walk. And he took him by the right hand, and lifted him up: and immediately his feet and ankle bones received strength. And he leaping up stood, and walked, and entered with them into the temple, walking, and leaping, and praising God. And all the people saw him walking and praising God: (Acts 4:6-8)

The people in the temple were astonished because they knew that this man was born lame. Seeing this man now walking and leaping "they were filled with wonder and amazement at what had happened to him." The people started to gather together in Solomon's Porch. Peter, taking advantage of the situation, began to preach his second Pentecost Sermon. He said, "Men of Israel, why do you marvel at this?" He explained that it was not through any power or godliness of their own that this great miracle happened. He very briefly showed the people how Jesus was glorified in the lives of Abraham, Isaac, and Jacob, showing them that Jesus was the same God who spoke through and worked in the lives of their forefathers.

Peter then preaches the Gospel in the synagogue.

And his name through faith in his name hath made this man strong, whom ye see and know: yea, the faith which is by him hath given him this perfect soundness in the presence of you all. And now, brethren, I wot that through ignorance ye did it, as did also your rulers. But those things, which God before had shewed by the mouth of all his prophets, that Christ should suffer, he hath so fulfilled. Repent ye therefore, and be converted, that your sins may be blotted out, when the times of refreshing shall come from the presence of the Lord; And he shall send Jesus Christ, which before was preached unto you: Whom the heaven must receive until the times of restitution of all things, which God hath spoken by the mouth of all his holy prophets since the world began. (Acts 3:16-21)

Peter boldly accused the Jews of having Jesus arrested and delivered up to be crucified, even though Pilate was determined to let Him go. They let a prisoner go free and killed the Prince of life who God had raised up from the dead. Peter continued by saying that it was through faith and power in Jesus name that miraculously healed this lame man. He told the people that he knows that they and their leaders crucified Jesus out of ignorance, and that all these things were prophesied by the Old Testament prophets, specifically that Jesus would suffer. God had fulfilled these prophecies. Having delivered the Gospel of the death, burial (*although not mentioned here*), and the resurrection of Jesus, he now told them what they must do, just like he told the men in Acts Chapter 2. Peter said:

Repent ye therefore, and be converted, that your sins may be blotted out, when the times of refreshing shall come from the presence of the Lord; And he shall send Jesus Christ, which before was preached unto you: (Acts 3:19-20)

When you break down what Peter said here, you will see a very similar reference to what he told the men on Pentecost Sunday when they asked, "What must we do?"

1. "Repent, and be converted." The very first words were exactly the same as on Pentecost. Translated from the Greek this means, "reconsider and convert, turn about" – this is repentance! [1]

2. "That your sins may be blotted out" in the Greek means "obliterate (*figuratively, pardon sin*): —blot out, wipe away. [2]

3. In Acts 2:38, Peter said, be baptized for the "remission of sins." That phrase is translated in the Greek: "pardon: —deliverance, forgiveness, liberty, remission." The two phrases are basically saying the same thing just in another way.

Therefore, according to these Scriptural accounts, when we repent and are baptized, God wipes our sins away, and the board is wiped clean! Tony Merida in Christ-Centered Exposition explains it this way:

Regarding the first, he says that through repentance, 'your sins may be wiped out' (v.19). This is a beautiful word picture. Parchment was expensive, so sometimes scribes used acid-free ink as they wrote on it. The ink just lay on top of the parchment, so a person could take a wet sponge and wipe a message away, blotting it out. To put Peter's point in modern terms, imagine having all your sins listed on a dry-eraser board. [3]

4. "When the times of refreshing shall come from the presence of the Lord" is a very interesting phrase because we see this term "refreshing" in a passage of Isaiah. These are the only two passages in the scripture where this word is used in the KJV.

For with stammering lips and another tongue will he speak to this people. To whom he said, This is the rest wherewith ye may cause the weary to rest; and this is the refreshing: yet they would not hear. (Isaiah 28:11-12)

The Times of Refreshing

In 1 Corinthians 14, Paul uses this verse in Isaiah to teach about speaking in tongues, more particularly, the "Gift of Tongues." Notice also that verse 20 in Acts 3 says, "And he shall send Jesus Christ, which before was preached unto you." How was Jesus Christ to be sent to them? The answer is as the Holy Ghost, which is the same way He filled believers in Acts Chapter 2. David Bernard writes:

> *In Acts 3:19 Peter preached, 'Repent ye therefore, and be converted, that your sins may be blotted out, when the times of refreshing shall come from the presence of the Lord.' The blotting out of sins includes water baptism (Acts 2:38; 22:16), and the times of refreshing refer to receiving the Holy Ghost with speaking in tongues (Isaiah 28:11-12).* [4]

What are these times of refreshing? Where do they come from? It is clear that the times of refreshing come from the presence of God in our lives. The events of Acts show us how to accomplish God's daily presence in our lives: through the infilling of the Holy Spirit. Stanley Horton writes in his commentary on Acts:

> *Repentance (a change of mind and attitude) and a turning to God will still bring times of refreshing from the presence of God. The day of spiritual blessing, the day of miracles, the day of revival, is not past. In the midst of terrible times we can still get our eyes on the Lord and receive mighty, refreshing outpourings of the Holy Spirit.* [5]

As Warren Doud explains Acts 3:19, we can see that turning to God brings about this supernatural refreshing:

> *Peter repeats the statement he made in Acts 2:38. God's plan calls for an instant change of attitude on their part. Their terrible guilt for their crime does not shut them out of God's grace, if they will turn to Christ. 'blotted out' – 'wiped out; erased; smeared out' Only found here and in Colossians*

2:14. Not 'when' the times of refreshing will come, ...' The times of refreshing are a result in a person's life which is brought about by repentance and turning to Christ. ⁶

Kenneth Gangel writes about the meaning of these times of refreshing:

Times of refreshing may come from the presence of the Lord - While this phrase clearly has eschatological overtones that will be fulfilled in the future when Israel as a nation repents (Zechariah 12:10-14 Zechariah 13:8-9, Romans 11:26), there is a sense in which it can be wonderfully applied to the life of every sinner who repents and believes the Gospel. And then as we are filled (Ephesians 5:18) and learn to walk by His Spirit (Galatians 5:16) we sense His presence, His face, unhindered by unconfessed sin and rebellion, and we are much more likely to experience times of refreshing, times of relief and rest for soul. ⁷

Ultimately, these times of refreshing come from Jesus himself:

Come unto me, all ye that labour and are heavy laden, and I will give you rest. Take my yoke upon you, and learn of me; for I am meek and lowly in heart: and ye shall find rest unto your souls. (Matthew 11:28-29)

When we repent, God will send Jesus Christ who Peter said has been "preached unto us" *(Acts 3:20)*. Now this scripture may be speaking of the second coming of Christ, but it was also preached by Jesus and the prophets that God's Spirit would be poured out in the latter days *(Joel 2:28; Jeremiah 31:33)*. What was it that Jesus told His Apostles about His going away? Did He not tell them that He would send them a Comforter?

Nevertheless, I tell you the truth; It is expedient for you that I go away: for if I go not away, the Comforter will not come unto you; but if I depart, I will send him unto you. (John 16:7)

And I will pray the Father, and he shall give you another Comforter, that he may abide with you for ever; (John 14:16)

But the Comforter, which is the Holy Ghost, whom the Father will send in my name, he shall teach you all things, and bring all things to your remembrance, whatsoever I have said unto you. (John 14:26)

Some may disagree with what I have written here, but since Peter preached the Gospel in Acts 2 and soon after that the lame man was healed, wouldn't Peter, after having preached the Gospel in Acts Chapter 3, have given his Jewish brethren (Pharisees and Sadducees) the same plan of salvation as he did to those on Pentecost *(Acts 2:38)*? If that is what Peter received from Jesus, why would he have changed the message in Acts Chapter 3? God's Word doesn't change from one chapter to another. Acts 2:38 is still the answer to all that ask, "What must I do to be saved?" Luke *(who wrote the Book of Acts)* just stated it a little differently so as not to be too repetitive because we will see it again in some of the other chapters.

This sending of Jesus Christ is the gift of the Holy Ghost, whom over 3000 people received on the Day of Pentecost. What Peter told the people in Acts 3:19 is very similar to what he preached to the people in Acts 2:38. Peter preached the gospel to the people and Acts 3:19 was what the response to the gospel should have been for those seeking salvation and the times of refreshing: Repentance, Baptism in Jesus Name, and receiving the Holy Ghost.

Although Jesus has been received back up into heaven until the restoration of all things, He has sent us His Spirit to remain with us forever and His Spirit will teach us all things that the Old Testament and New Testament Prophets have spoken. This includes the Revelation of Jesus Christ that the Apostle John received in visions, which tells us the end of all things. Jesus will physically remain in Heaven until He is ready to set up His Kingdom during the Millennial reign of Jesus Christ. Stanley Horton says in his Commentary of Acts:

From this passage we see that repentance and a radical turning to God bring not only obliteration of sins but 'times of refreshing' (v.19) from the Lord. Nor do we have to wait until Jesus comes back before we can enjoy these seasons of revival and blessing. We can have such times now, and as the Greek especially indicates, we can have them until Jesus comes back to earth again. [8]

Dean Pinter remarks:

In the present, however, a foretaste of the future is anticipated in the "times of refreshing." The advance anticipation, Peter declares in this passage (Acts 3:19), can be received when people turn away from their wickedness and turn to the Lord in the present. [9]

And when they do repent of their sins, they receive the Holy Ghost just like the 120 did on the Day of Pentecost, speaking in unknown tongues as the Spirit of God gives the utterance. This is the season that we are living in right now. Anyone who is willing to repent and turn away from sin can receive this precious gift of God's Holy Spirit. We are living very close to the day when the Lord is expected to come back to this earth, and it is in these last days that we will need His Holy Spirit to lead and guide us through the perilous times that are coming upon us, as recorded in the Books of Daniel and Revelation.

Jesus is That Prophet

For Moses truly said unto the fathers, A prophet shall the Lord your God raise up unto you of your brethren, like unto me; him shall ye hear in all things whatsoever he shall say unto you. And it shall come to pass, that every soul, which will not hear that prophet, shall be destroyed from among the people. Yea, and all the prophets from Samuel and those that follow after, as many as have spoken, have likewise foretold of these days. Ye are the children of the prophets, and of the covenant which God made with our fathers, saying unto Abraham, And in thy seed shall all the kindreds of the earth be blessed. Unto you first God, having raised up his Son Jesus, sent him to bless you, in turning away every one of you from his iniquities. (Acts 3:22)

As Peter continues his message to the Jewish people in the Temple, he reminds them of what the Prophet Moses told the people before he died (*Deuteronomy 18:15*). Jesus is that Prophet that God raised up who came into this world.

He was in the world, and the world was made by him, and the world knew him not. He came unto his own, and his own received him not. But as many as received him, to them gave he power to become the sons of God, even to them that believe on his name: Which were born, not of blood, nor of the will of the flesh, nor of the will of man, but of God. (John 1:10-13)

For Moses said, 'The Lord your God will raise up for you a prophet like me from among your own people; you must listen to everything he tells you. Anyone who does not listen to him will be completely cut off from among his people. (Acts 3:22-23 NIV)

Peter delivered to his Jewish brethren everything that Jesus gave him to tell the people in the Great Commission. Those who don't obey the teaching of the Apostle's doctrine, as the scripture says, they will suffer the consequences.

This great New Testament salvation was offered to the Jews first, but it was not God's plan for this to remain just among the Jewish nation. The Samaritans (*half Jews/half Gentile*) in Acts chapter 8 are offered this gift of God, followed by the Gentiles in Acts chapter 10. This is the fulfillment of the promise that God made to Abraham that "in thee shall all families of the earth be blessed" (*Gen 12:3*). God's plan of salvation today is for *whosoever will believe.* As the Apostle Paul started his missionary journeys he always went into the synagogues and spoke to the Jews first, but when they rejected the Word of God, Paul went to the Gentiles who gladly received him.

Peter and John Before the Council

> *And as they spake unto the people, the priests, and the captain of the temple, and the Sadducees, came upon them, Being grieved that they taught the people, and preached through Jesus the resurrection from the dead. And they laid hands on them, and put them in hold unto the next day: for it was now eventide. Howbeit many of them which heard the word believed; and the number of the men was about five thousand. (Acts 4:1-4)*

As the fourth chapter of Acts begins, we start to see a resistance, by the religious authorities, against the Apostles and their message, especially regarding the name of Jesus and the resurrection from the dead. This chapter also records the first imprisonment of the Apostles after the death of Jesus. Picking up from where chapter 3 left off, as Peter continued to speak to the people, the priests, the temple captain, and the Sadducees were all grieved about what Peter was preaching. He was not preaching that Jesus had risen from the dead (*although that point did get across*), but he was teaching the people that through Jesus there is a resurrection of the dead (*Acts 4:2 NLT*). The reason the Sadducees were grieved was due to the fact that they didn't believe or teach about the resurrection from the dead. Now Peter and John were powerfully proclaiming that Jesus had risen, and they were filling the minds and hearts of the people with this truth and the number of believers had increased to five thousand, not including the women and children. It is obvious that the Sadducees were troubled by Peter's preaching of the resurrection and the healing of the lame man. Peter's preaching of the resurrection exposed the lie of the Jewish leaders that the disciples came by night and stole His body. The truth was now out in the open.

The Gospel of Matthew is the only Gospel that reveals the cover up of how the Jewish priests had bribed the Roman soldiers to try to deny Jesus' resurrection.

Now when they were going, behold, some of the watch came into the city, and shewed unto the chief priests all the things that were done. And when they were assembled with the elders, and had taken counsel, they gave large money unto the soldiers, Saying, Say ye, His disciples came by night, and stole him away while we slept. And if this come to the governor's ears, we will persuade him, and secure you. So they took the money and did as they were taught: and this saying is commonly reported among the Jews until this day. (Matthew 28:11-15)

It was obvious to these priests and the Sadducees that a notable miracle had taken place since all the people knew this man was lame from birth, which was about forty years. During Jesus' ministry on earth, these same "religious leaders" refused to recognize anything Jesus did even after He raised Lazarus who had been dead for four days. Now their problem was only multiplied because instead of having just Jesus performing miracles and preaching the gospel, you now have the apostles and others ministering the Word and performing miracles in Jesus' Name.

The Apostles Peter and John, as the scripture says, "were put in hold" (*Acts 4:3*) until the next day. The hold was basically a prison where they were kept, for the Sadducees and the priests didn't know what to do with them. There was no doubt that a miracle had been performed, but the Jewish leaders did not want to recognize it because then they would be admitting that the miracle was done by the Apostles, in the name of Jesus. However, they also couldn't deny it, because all the people in the Temple saw the blind beggar walking, leaping, and praising God. This was the same problem the Jewish leaders encountered when they wanted to arrest Jesus for the miracles He did. They were always afraid that the people would revolt against them. That is why they arrested Jesus at night when no one was around.

The problem for the religious leaders was also escalating because, due to the miracle of the lame man, the number of people who believed rose to five thousand. Besides the miracle, Peter had been preaching the truth about the resurrection of Jesus Christ, and now these new believers were being taught the very thing the Jewish leaders tried to hide from them. The Greek phrase for "about five-thousand" means "as it were" or "approximately." [10] There are those that believe that the number rose to 5000, being an increase from the Day of Pentecost outpouring, while others believe that these were in addition to the Day of Pentecost.

Peter and John Before the High Priest

> *And it came to pass on the morrow, that their rulers, and elders, and scribes, And Annas the high priest, and Caiaphas, and John, and Alexander, and as many as were of the kindred of the high priest, were gathered together at Jerusalem. And when they had set them in the midst, they asked, By what power, or by what name, have ye done this? Then Peter, filled with the Holy Ghost, said unto them, Ye rulers of the people, and elders of Israel, If we this day be examined of the good deed done to the impotent man, by what means he is made whole; Be it known unto you all, and to all the people of Israel, that by the name of Jesus Christ of Nazareth, whom ye crucified, whom God raised from the dead, even by him doth this man stand here before you whole. This is the stone which was set at nought of you builders, which is become the head of the corner. Neither is there salvation in any other: for there is none other name under heaven given among men, whereby we must be saved. (Acts 4:5-12)*

On the next morning, the Jewish rulers along with the High Priest and their brethren gathered together to question Peter and John about the miracle of the lame man. They demanded of Peter and John to know by who or what power, had this man been healed? Horton believes that when these leaders said "What" (*power or Name*), they were speaking contemptuously or asking in a derogatory way since these Apostles were just unschooled or ordinary men; (*those not trained in their schools*). This question just gave Peter another opportunity to preach to them the gospel of Jesus Christ. The scripture says that Peter was filled with the Holy Ghost. Stanley Horton writes about this:

The form of the Greek word here indicates a new, fresh filling. This does not mean he had lost any of the power and presence of the Spirit he received on the Day of Pentecost...the Lord simply enlarged his capacity... to meet this new need for power to witness. [11]

Being filled with the Holy Ghost, Peter was not to be intimidated by the Jewish leaders' tactics. This is exactly what Jesus meant when He told His Apostles that He would be with them and would give them the words to say in Luke 12:

And when they bring you unto the synagogues, and unto magistrates, and powers, take ye no thought how or what thing ye shall answer, or what ye shall say: For the Holy Ghost shall teach you in the same hour what ye ought to say. (Luke 12:11-12)

He continued by saying, if you are asking me how this lame man was made whole, "Be it known unto you all, and to all the people of Israel, that by the name of Jesus Christ of Nazareth, whom ye crucified, whom God raised from the dead, *even* by him doth this man stand here before you whole" (*Acts 4:10*). Dean Pinter says this about Peter's response:

He also adds a phrase that was sure not to endear himself to his audience: 'Whom you crucified but whom God raised from the dead (4:10)'. Not only was this phrase theologically offensive to the Sadducees, who did not believe in the resurrection, but it also implicates the leaders in an act of injustice in handing Jesus over to the Romans to be executed. [12]

Peter explains that Jesus was the One who was rejected of the High Priest, the Pharisees, and the Sadducees. His Words and His teachings were not received by them. Though He was rejected by the Jewish leaders and cast aside, God had highly exalted Him and made Him the head or chief cornerstone of His New Testament Church! Peter personalized Psalm 118:12 to be directed to these Jewish leaders when he said:

This is the stone which was set at nought of you builders, which is become the head of the corner. (Psalm 118:12)

The Exclusiveness of Jesus' Name

Peter, in his next statement, declares that there is salvation in no other but the Lord Jesus Christ. He is the One that came down from Heaven to bring salvation to all men. He was the Jewish Messiah, but the leaders rejected Him. How could the Pharisees, Sadducees, and the Sanhedrin not have understood that Jesus was their Messiah? They had all the prophecies of the Old Testament, even the prophecy of Daniel and the seventy weeks, which if they had bothered to study, they would have known about the time that their Messiah would be on the earth. How true are the words in the Gospel of John?

He was in the world, and the world was made by him, and the world knew him not. He came unto his own, and his own received him not. But as many as received him, to them gave he power to become the sons of God, even to them that believe on his name: Which were born, not of blood, nor of the will of the flesh, nor of the will of man, but of God. (John 1:10-13)

Though the Jewish leaders refused to receive Him, those who did believe on His name, were born again. This was not a birth through a natural blood line or a birth by human decision, but it is a birth from above: the New Birth recording in John 3:3-5. The Life Application Bible Commentary states:

The new birth cannot be attained by an act of human will, and it has absolutely nothing to do with human planning. It is a gift of God. [13]

Peter astounds the Jewish leaders and answers their question in verse 7, "By what power or what name have you done this?" Peter lets all these Jewish leaders understand that outside of Jesus they will never find salvation, for there is no other name, given under heaven, given among men, whereby we must be saved" (*Acts 4:12*). That word *must* is from the Greek word *"die,"* and it means: "necessary (*as binding*):—behooved, be meet, must (*needs*), (be) need(*-ful*), ought, should" (*Strongs Greek definition 1163*). According to the Complete Word Study Dictionary, New Testament:

> *In Acts 4:12 there is only one way whereby it is inevitable for people to be saved. Here the inevitability is not inferring that all will be saved, but propounds the necessity of the method whereby someone may be saved.* [14]

This means that there is salvation in Jesus Christ and in Him alone. How this must have angered the Sadducees because first, they didn't believe in Jesus, and secondly, their faith was totally based in the Old Testament scriptures, especially the Pentateuch, the first five books of the Old Testament.

Peter was telling us of the importance of the Name of Jesus. When Peter preached his first Pentecost sermon he said, "Repent and be baptized every one of you in the Name of Jesus Christ, for the remission of sins." The Apostle Paul said in Colossians chapter 3: "And whatsoever ye do in word or deed, do all in the name of the Lord Jesus, giving thanks to God and the Father by him" (*Colossians 3:17*).

In the biblical record of the New Testament regarding baptism, people were baptized in no other name but the Name of Jesus.

1. The Acts 2:38 records: "...be baptized every one of you in the name of Jesus Christ for the remission of sins."
2. In Samaria, Philip went down to preach the word and we are told that the believers hadn't received the Holy Ghost (interesting that they didn't receive it when they first believed) but "only they were baptized in the name of the Lord Jesus." *(Acts 8:16)*
3. Cornelius and all his household received the Holy Ghost when Peter preached to him and then Peter commanded

them to be baptized and when they were, he baptized them in the "Name of the Lord." *(Acts 10:48)*
4. Paul at Ephesus met some disciples of John the Baptist and he asked them about their baptism. They told him that they were baptized unto repentance by John. Paul then told them about Jesus and: "When they heard this, they were baptized in the name of the Lord Jesus." *(Acts 19:5)*
5. In Acts Chapter 22 we read of the baptism of the Apostle Paul. This is the Apostle's own account of his baptism. "And now why tarriest thou? arise, and be baptized, and wash away thy sins, calling on the name of the Lord." *(Acts 22:16)*

Even according to history, Jesus Name Baptism was the only baptism for the first 100 years.

1. *Britannica Encyclopedia, 11th Edition, Volume 3, page 365 – Baptism was changed from the name of Jesus to words Father, Son & Holy Ghost in 2nd Century.*
2. *Canney Encyclopedia of Religion, page 53 – The early church baptized in the name of the Lord Jesus until the second century.*
3. *Hastings Encyclopedia of Religion, Volume 2 – Christian baptism was administered using the words, "in the name of Jesus." page 377. Baptism was always in the name of Jesus until the time of Justin Martyr, page 389.*
4. *Catholic Encyclopedia, Volume 2, page 263 – Here the authors acknowledged that the baptismal formula was changed by their church.*
5. *Schaff – Herzog Religious Encyclopedia, Volume 1, page 435 – The New Testament knows only the baptism in the name of Jesus*
6. *Hastings Dictionary of Bible, page 88 – It must be acknowledged that the three-fold name of Matthew 28:19 does not appear to have been used by the primitive church, but rather in the name of Jesus, Jesus Christ, or Lord Jesus.*

Even Wikipedia records that Jesus Name baptism was the baptism of the early church:

> *The first baptisms in early Christianity are recorded in the Acts of the Apostles. Acts 2 records the Apostle Peter, on the day of Pentecost, preaching to the crowds to "repent and be baptized in the name of Jesus Christ for the remission (or forgiveness) of sins" (Acts 2:3<u>8</u>). Other detailed records of baptisms in the Book of Acts show the first Apostles baptizing in the name of Jesus. The Apostle Paul also refers to baptism into Christ Jesus.* [15]

The Apostle Paul brings out the importance of Baptism in Jesus name when he said:

> *Know ye not, that so many of us as were baptized into Jesus Christ were baptized into his death? Therefore, we are buried with him by baptism into death: that like as Christ was raised up from the dead by the glory of the Father, even so we also should walk in newness of life. For if we have been planted together in the likeness of his death, we shall be also in the likeness of his resurrection: (Romans 6:3-5)*

We not only die with Him in repentance, but we are buried with Him in Baptism so that we may be raised from the dead to walk in newness of life. So, all we who are in Christ are new creations.

> *Therefore, if any man be in Christ, he is a new creature: old things are passed away; behold, all things are become new. (2 Corinthians 5:17)*

Not in the New Testament scripture, nor in the historical record of the first century is there any record of anyone being baptized in any other name except the name of Jesus. So why today do most Christian organizations baptize in the name (*titles*) of the Father, Son, and Holy Ghost? Are you baptized in the only name given among men, whereby we *must* be saved?

The members of the council were amazed when they saw the

boldness of Peter and John, and they realized that they were unlearned men and had no special training in the scriptures. However, they also recognize them as men who had been with Jesus. The council was amazed at what being with Jesus had done for them. That is such an awesome compliment. But since they could see the man who had been healed standing right in front of them, there was nothing that the council could say so they ordered Peter and John out of the council chamber and conferred among themselves. They asked each other the question "What should we do with these men?" *(Acts 4:16)*

Although they couldn't deny that an absolute miracle had taken place, they warned the Apostles not to speak to anyone in Jesus' name, trying to keep them from spreading their "propaganda" any further. But Peter and John replied, "You decide whether we should obey God rather than you. For we just cannot stop telling everybody everything we have seen and heard" *(Acts 4:19-20)*. As soon as they were freed, they gathered together with other believers, and they were joined together in prayer.

And when they had prayed, the place was shaken where they were assembled together; and they were all filled with the Holy Ghost, and they spake the word of God with boldness. (Acts 4:31)

The Apostles prayed until they were renewed or refilled with the power and anointing of the Holy Ghost. They will need this as they will be brought in question before the Jewish Council again in Chapter 5.

Acts Chapter 5

Due to the death of Ananias and Sapphira great fear came upon all the church and upon all those who heard these things *(vs 11)*. Peter was evidently operating under the Gifts of the Holy Spirit at this time since no one but Ananias, Sapphira, and God knew that they had lied to the Holy Ghost concerning the sale of their home. Besides these things the scripture tells us that many signs and wonders were done by the hand of the Apostles and many people believed and were added to the Lord.

> *And believers were the more added to the Lord, multitudes both of men and women. Insomuch that they brought forth the sick into the streets, and laid them on beds and couches, that at the least the shadow of Peter passing by might overshadow some of them. There came also a multitude out of the cities round about unto Jerusalem, bringing sick folks, and them which were vexed with unclean spirits: and they were healed everyone. (Acts 5:14-16)*

What a testimony of the power of God working through the Apostles! For the scripture said that even the shadow of Peter passing by them might overshadow some of them that they might be healed. People also came from out of the nearby cities and all-around Jerusalem bringing sick folks and those that were possessed of unclean spirits, and each one of them were healed. But the next day the Sadducees had Peter and John arrested and put into prison. That night an angel of the Lord opened the prison doors and brought the Apostles out telling them to: "Go, stand and speak in the temple to the people all the words of this life" (*Acts 5:20*).

When the Apostles heard this, they went into the temple early in the morning and began to teach. Meanwhile, the high priest and the council with all the elders sent men to the prison to have the Apostles brought out to them. But when they searched the prison, the Apostles were not to be found there. Someone came and told them that the Apostles were in the Temple teaching the people. Then the captain and the officers came and brought them out peacefully before the council because they were afraid of the people. As they were standing before the High Priest, he asked them:

> *Saying, Did not we straitly command you that ye should not teach in this name? and, behold, ye have filled Jerusalem with your doctrine, and intend to bring this man's blood upon us. (Acts 5:28)*

To this the Apostles answered:

Then Peter and the other apostles answered and said, We ought to obey God rather than men. The God of our fathers raised up Jesus, whom ye slew and hanged on a tree. Him hath God exalted with his right hand to be a Prince and a Saviour, for to give repentance to Israel, and forgiveness of sins. And we are his witnesses of these things; and so is also the Holy Ghost, whom God hath given to them that obey him. (Acts 5:29-32)

Let us look a little closer at the answer of the Apostles. They made the High Priest realize that there is a higher power that they answer to when they said, "We ought to obey God rather than men." God and the will of God should have been what the High Priest also wanted, but they had long ago departed from the true path. Boldly then, the Apostles accused these religious leaders of crucifying Jesus upon a tree but telling them that God had exalted him with power (*right hand*) to be a Prince and Savior. Notice, He would give repentance to Israel, and forgiveness of sins (*remission of sins at baptism*) and God would give the Holy Ghost to them that obey Him.

This is the same answer that Peter gave on Pentecost Sunday. People who obey the gospel must repent, be baptized in Jesus' Name and receive the gift of the Holy Ghost, with the evidence of speaking in unknown tongues as they did on the day of Pentecost, and at other times, as we will see again in Chapters 8, 10, and 19 and also in other places throughout the Book of Acts. There is a pattern in the Book of Acts that shows us how we must be saved. Many pastors, teachers, commentators, and Bible scholars ignore this and will consistently point people to Acts 16 where Paul said to the Philippian jailor, "Believe on the Lord Jesus Christ, and thou shalt be saved, and thy house." They will also point people to Romans 10:

That if thou shalt confess with thy mouth the Lord Jesus, and shalt believe in thine heart that God hath raised him from the dead, thou shalt be saved. (Romans 10:9)

I do believe both Acts 16 and Romans 10, however I do not just stop at believing. Many pastors and teachers think that saying that we must repent, be baptized, and receive the Holy Ghost is a form of works. Ask yourselves the question, "Can you be saved without obeying the gospel? The answer to that is no! My faith in the work of Jesus Christ on the cross will lead me to obey the Gospel message and respond by way of Acts 2:38 and many other passages that speak of the same thing. David Bernard writes:

We appropriate or apply that gospel to our lives by repentance (death to sin), water baptism (burial), and the Spirit baptism (new life in Christ), thereby identifying personally with the redemptive purpose of Christ. [16]

James writes in his Epistle:

Even so faith, if it hath not works, is dead, being alone. Yea, a man may say, Thou hast faith, and I have works: shew me thy faith without thy works, and I will shew thee my faith by my works. (James 2:17-18)

Final Thoughts

There is such an urgency for a revival of the true Pentecostal experience today, for the end of the Church age is swiftly coming upon us and the Lord is coming back very soon to set up His glorious Kingdom! Jesus once wept over Jerusalem because He knew that His own Jewish people had rejected Him, and they would go through terrible tribulation because of it. He said that they knew not the time of their visitation. Today God is visiting with us and calling us to obey His Gospel.

It's not my place to criticize or judge anyone who disagrees with my interpretation of the scriptures. I am just letting people know what the scripture says, and each one must make up their own mind whether to accept it or reject it. Let us remember that this is the time of our visitation!

7
ON TO THE GENTILES

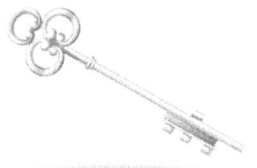

Most people don't like to feel different. Differences attract attention, and it is not always good attention. When I was a young boy of only five years old, I discovered that I was born into a family of Italian descent. My mom and dad were both born in Brooklyn, N.Y. in the early nineteen hundreds. My grandparents on both sides were born in Italy and migrated to the States by boat and came through Ellis Island. My fathers' parents were from Naples and mother's family was from Sicily. My parents were very proud of their Italian heritage, but I didn't care that much about it. As far as I was concerned, I am an American. I had no desire to travel to Italy, and I had no desire to learn the Italian language.

Then I learned about a man named Cornelius. He is found in the Bible in Acts 10, and guess what? He is a Roman Centurion who commanded a company of about one hundred men, called the Italian band, and he was a Gentile. Cornelius was such a devout and godly man, that he got God's attention. The lives of multitudes of Gentile converts like Cornelius (and my family) would be given access to God's Kingdom through the New Birth. And it began one day as recorded in Acts 10. Praise be to God!!

Jesus Set the Stage

Before the events in the Book of Acts, Jesus metaphorically set the stage for his apostles, leading by example. His mission was to break the yoke of sin for every man, regardless of creed or background. He accomplished this in the following ways:

1. He ate with publicans and sinners, even going so far as to forgive the thief on the cross.
2. He waited for the woman at the well, knowing she was an outcast and Samaritan.
3. He healed the Centurion's daughter because of the Centurion's faith (the Centurion was a Gentile).
4. He taught the disciples an important lesson through the parable of the Good Samaritan.

Jesus Entrusts Peter with the Keys to the Kingdom

God had poured out His Holy Spirit on the Day of Pentecost and all the recipients at that time were Jews. Peter had been given the Keys to the Kingdom of God when it was revealed to him that Jesus was the Son of God. Jesus had asked His disciples, "Who do men say that I the Son of Man am?" *(Matt 16:13)*. Jesus may have asked this question because He wanted to know what those in other cities and towns thought about Him. His disciples would have had the opportunity to talk to more people than He Himself would have. The disciples responded by saying, "Some say you are John the Baptist: some Elijah; Jeremiah, or one of the prophets" *(Matt 16:14)*. Jesus asks the question again but with a little different twist this time. He asks His disciples, "Who do you say I am?" *(Matt 16:15)*. This was the question that brought about Simon Peter's answer in Matthew chapter 16.

> *"And Simon Peter answered and said, Thou art the Christ, the Son of the living God." (Matthew 16:16)*

Peter had just declared that Jesus was the Messiah. Peter didn't say this of his own accord. It wasn't through his own flesh and blood that he envisioned this, but this was revealed to Him from above, from God. To Peter's answer, Jesus responded by saying:

> *And I say also unto thee, That thou art Peter, and upon this rock I will build my church; and the gates of hell shall not prevail against it. And I will give unto thee the keys of the kingdom of heaven: and whatsoever thou shalt bind on earth shall be bound in heaven: and whatsoever thou shalt loose on earth shall be loosed in heaven. (Matthew 16:18-19)*

The Significance of the Keys

Keys are symbols of authority. Keys are used to open and shut things. According to the website "Thehistoryofkeys.com," it states:

> *History of keys started at the same moment when first locks appeared in **ancient Babylon and Egypt**, some 6 thousand years ago. These simple wooden devices used small pins which were hidden in a small opening near the bolt. By using wooden toothbrush-shaped key, Egyptians could lift those small pins and unlock the blot.* [1]

The one who has the keys has the power to open and to shut. In the context of this scripture, Peter is given the keys because of his confession of faith that Jesus was the Christ, the Anointed One. He would be the one that would open the door to the Kingdom of God, not only for the Jews *(Acts 2)*, or Samaritans *(Acts 8)*, but also to the Gentile world *(Acts 10)*. This would fulfill God's promise to Abraham that, "in thee shall ALL families of the earth be blessed" *(Gen 12:3)*. David Bernard explains the importance of these keys:

> *The keys of the Kingdom, however, refers to the power to open the Kingdom of God to the world through preaching. By giving Peter the keys, Jesus acknowledged that Peter would possess the true salvation message. By this*

message, people could enter into the Kingdom of God. The specific appointment of Peter apparently signified the vital role Peter would play in introducing the gospel to all classes of people at Pentecost...What message did Peter use to open the door of the New Testament church to the Jews, Samaritans, and Gentiles? At Pentecost he proclaimed "Repent, and be baptized everyone of you in the name of Jesus Christ for the remission of sins, and he shall receive the gift of the Holy Ghost. [2]

Cornelius

There was a certain man in Caesarea called Cornelius, a centurion of the band called the Italian band, A devout man, and one that feared God with all his house, which gave much alms to the people, and prayed to God alway. He saw in a vision evidently about the ninth hour of the day an angel of God coming in to him, and saying unto him, Cornelius. And when he looked on him, he was afraid, and said, What is it, Lord? And he said unto him, Thy prayers and thine alms are come up for a memorial before God. And now send men to Joppa, and call for one Simon, whose surname is Peter: He lodgeth with one Simon a tanner, whose house is by the sea side: he shall tell thee what thou oughtest to do. (Acts 10:1-6)

We are not really sure as to the timing of this chapter compared with Acts 2, the first Pentecost Sunday. After Stephen's death in Acts 7, persecution scattered the Christians to different places fulfilling what Jesus told the Apostles just before He ascended into heaven.

But ye shall receive power, after that the Holy Ghost is come upon you: and ye shall be witnesses unto me both in Jerusalem, and in all Judaea, and in Samaria, and unto the uttermost part of the earth. (Acts 1:8)

Philip went down to the city of Samaria and started to preach the gospel in that city. We read the account of what happened there in Acts 8 which we will examine in a later chapter. After Saul of Tarsus was converted and the persecution stopped, the scripture says:

Then had the churches rest throughout all Judaea and Galilee and Samaria and were edified; and walking in the fear of the Lord, and in the comfort of the Holy Ghost, were multiplied. (Acts 9:31)

We then find Peter in the city of Lydda where he performed a miracle, healing a man that was sick of the palsy *(Acts 9:33)*. He then went down to Joppa where he worked another miracle, this time raising a woman named Tabitha from the dead *(Acts 9:40)*. Joppa was an ancient port city in Israel, a place where people and merchandise can enter or leave a country. The ninth chapter of Acts ends with Peter staying many days in the house of Simon the Tanner *(Acts 9:43)*. This is the setting for chapter 10.

As this chapter opens, we see a man named Cornelius, a Gentile, who lives in a city called Caesarea. Caesarea Maritima was a major seaport about 60 miles northwest of Jerusalem and it functioned as the provincial capital of Judea and was home to the Roman governors [3]. "Cornelius was a rather common Latin name. He was a fairly wealthy man of status living in this beautiful city" [4]. According to the scripture, Cornelius was a devout man who feared God, "…In other words, he was right in his attitudes toward both God and people and by grace was living a godly life" [5]. He also gave much alms, and had a consistent prayer life.

Cornelius was a Centurion, and Centurions were to be men who were "good leaders of steady and prudent mind" [6]. Another source explains: "Most God-fearing men, like Cornelius, participated in synagogue worship and often became patrons and supporters for the synagogue communities" [7]. But Cornelius was seeking God with his whole heart, and it was to such a man that God sent an angel to tell him what he needed to do to be saved. In the ninth hour of the day, an angel appears to Cornelius and tells him that his prayers came up as a memorial before God.

What could it mean when it says that Cornelius' prayers came up as a Memorial before God? We see offerings of memorials in the Old Testament.

> *And he shall bring it to Aaron's sons the priests: and he shall take thereout his handful of the flour thereof, and of the oil thereof, with all the frankincense thereof; and the priest shall burn the memorial of it upon the altar, to be an offering made by fire, of a sweet savour unto the LORD: (Leviticus 2:2)*

The priest takes only a handful of the meal offering and burns it on the altar. The scripture says that the priest shall burn the memorial upon the altar. According to the Story of God Commentary:

> *This was a share of the grain harvest that symbolically reminded Israel that the entire harvest was God's... In using a memorial offering to refer to Cornelius' prayers and good deeds, this might be indicative of the gentile 'harvest' of souls to come.* [8]

The angel instructs him to send for Peter who was staying in Joppa and he tells him the exact location where Peter is lodging *(Acts 10:6)*. You talk about a GPS system! The angel said that Peter will tell him what he ought to do. It is very interesting that although Cornelius was devout and believed in the True God of the Jews, he was a man who prayed and gave generously, yet he was not saved. No works can save a person. If we will come to God, as Jesus told Nicodemus, we *must* be born again. Although the angel came and gave Cornelius direction for what he needed to do if he wanted to be saved, the angel did not preach the gospel to him. That is because the Great Commission to preach the death, burial, and resurrection of Jesus Christ is given to men, and not to angels.

Peter's Vision on the Roof Top

> *And when the angel which spake unto Cornelius was departed, he called two of his household servants, and a devout soldier of them that waited on him continually; And when he had declared all these things unto them, he sent them to Joppa. On the morrow, as they went on their journey, and*

drew nigh unto the city, Peter went up upon the housetop to pray about the sixth hour: And he became very hungry, and would have eaten: but while they made ready, he fell into a trance, And saw heaven opened, and a certain vessel descending unto him, as it had been a great sheet knit at the four corners, and let down to the earth: Wherein were all manner of four-footed beasts of the earth, and wild beasts, and creeping things, and fowls of the air. And there came a voice to him, Rise, Peter; kill, and eat. But Peter said, Not so, Lord; for I have never eaten any thing that is common or unclean. And the voice spake unto him again the second time, What God hath cleansed, that call not thou common. This was done thrice: and the vessel was received up again into heaven. Now while Peter doubted in himself what this vision which he had seen should mean, behold, the men which were sent from Cornelius had made inquiry for Simon's house, and stood before the gate, And called, and asked whether Simon, which was surnamed Peter, were lodged there. (Acts 10:7-18)

Upon the angel's departure, Cornelius called his trusted servants and sent them to Joppa in search of the Apostle Peter. As Cornelius' servants came in close proximity of the city, Peter goes up to the rooftop to pray, about the 6th hour (*12 noon*). Some of the homes in those days had flat roofs which can be accessed through an outdoor stairway. Peter probably went up there to find a place where he could pray uninterruptedly [9]. While Peter was waiting for food to be prepared, he became very hungry and fell into a trance. Horton tells us:

This does not mean a trance in the modern sense of the word, however; nor does it imply a hypnotic state. It simply means his mind was distracted from whatever he was thinking about as he sensed something important was about to happen. [10]

The Complete Word Study Dictionary New Testament explains Peter's experience as:

A trance, sacred ecstasy or rapture of the mind beyond itself when the use of external senses are suspended and God reveals something in a peculiar manner.' [11]

Another explanation by the Zondervan Illustrated Bible Backgrounds Commentary of Peter's experience is:

The term literally means 'to stand outside yourself' and refers to a state of being brought about by God 'in which consciousness is wholly or partially suspended. [12]

During this trance Peter saw heaven opened and what looked like a great sheet coming down out of heaven. There were all manner of four-footed beasts of the earth and wild beasts, reptiles, creeping things, and fowls of the air in that sheet. All of a sudden, a voice said to Peter, "Rise, Peter; kill, and eat." Now this must have been repulsive to a true Jewish person. The Old Testament law prohibited Israel from eating these kinds of animals and Peter, being a devout Jew, said to the Lord that he had never eaten anything that was common or unclean. He would never defile himself by eating anything that would cause him to become ceremonially unclean. The voice spoke again saying, "What God hath cleansed, *that* call not thou common" *(Acts 10:15)*. This happened three times and then the sheet was received back into heaven.

This needed to happen to help Peter overcome his strong prejudice about dealing with Gentiles. During that time, Gentiles were considered to be unclean, mainly because they were uncircumcised, and the Jew was to have no dealings with them. So, Jesus caused Peter to fall into that trance to help him to realize that God wanted to save Gentiles too. Now while Peter was trying to figure out what this was all about, Cornelius' servants came to the house and asked if Simon Peter was staying there. M.D. Treece tells us of the Jewish prejudices against the Gentiles during the first century:

> When the Lord began the inclusion of Gentiles into the Gospel, he chose those who were Gentiles in the purest sense of the word. Whereas Samaria was half Jewish, these Romans were not in any way related to their worship, except as they became proselytes. Not only were the Romans looked upon as foreigners, but their presence was greatly resented by all the Jews. Roman domination has penetrated every facet of Jewish life, especially religion, and was acutely felt by the monotheistic Jew. This expansion of the gospel to Romans required such a drastic change in evangelism that extraordinary communications from the Lord were essential. [13]

Peter no doubt had strong feelings about these Gentiles, especially because they were often the oppressor of the Jewish people. Stanley Horton writes in his commentary on Acts:

> It was obvious from the beginning of the Church that being converted to Christ and even being baptized in the Holy Spirit did not automatically remove the prejudices people had grown up with... Many laws and customs separated Jews from Gentiles, especially the dietary laws. Nor would any Jew eat food prepared by a Gentile, for he believed this too would make him unclean. For the Jerusalem church Jesus' words recorded in John 3:16 did not apply to Gentiles; consequently they made no provision for fellowship with Gentiles who did not first come under the law and consent to circumcision. So, the Holy Spirit had to deal with Peter to remove his prejudice and then enable him to use the keys (Matt 16:19) to open 'the door to Rome and the Gentiles.' [14]

This explains why Jesus gave Peter the vision of the sheet coming down from heaven with all kinds of unclean animals in it. It could also be the reason why God poured out His Spirit on the Gentiles before Peter even finished preaching to them.

Peter Goes with Cornelius' Men

> *While Peter thought on the vision, the Spirit said unto him, Behold, three men seek thee. Arise therefore, and get thee down, and go with them, doubting nothing: for I have sent them. Then Peter went down to the men which were sent unto him from Cornelius; and said, Behold, I am he whom ye seek: what is the cause wherefore ye are come? And they said, Cornelius the centurion, a just man, and one that feareth God, and of good report among all the nation of the Jews, was warned from God by an holy angel to send for thee into his house, and to hear words of thee. Then called he them in, and lodged them. And on the morrow Peter went away with them, and certain brethren from Joppa accompanied him. (Acts 10:19-23)*

As Peter pondered what this vision could mean, the Holy Ghost spoke to him and said, three men have come looking for you. Get up, go downstairs, and go with them without hesitation. Don't worry, for I have sent them" *(Acts 10:19-20)*. When Peter met the men of Cornelius' household, he asked them the reason why they were looking for him. The men told Peter that their master, who is a devout man and has good report among the Jewish people was warned by God to send for him to "hear words of thee" *(Acts 10:22)*. Peter then lodged the men for the night. According to Jewish tradition, there were risks with hosting Gentiles in one's home. Many considered it a defilement.

This is probably something Peter would not have done except that the Lord had spoken to him about the three visitors. When morning had come, Peter went with them, taking six men *(Acts 11:12)* of Joppa with him, Jewish men, because he knew other Jewish believers would question him on going into a Gentile home.

Cornelius was all set and waiting for Peter's arrival. He had called members of his family and friends so that they also could hear the words Peter was going to say. As Peter enters the house, Cornelius falls down at Peter's feet and begins to worship him. As explained in Zondervan Illustrated Bible Backgrounds Commentary:

> *In Near Eastern cultures, prostrating oneself before a king or superior is a sign of great respect. Cornelius probably looked on Peter as a divine messenger, an angel.* [15]

However, Peter immediately stopped him, telling him, "Stand up, I also am just a man" *(Acts 10:25)*. Now as Peter goes into the house, he saw all the people there. I believe it started to dawn on him that God was about to do something that will astound him. So, Peter asked Cornelius for the reason that he had called for him. And this was Cornelius' answer:

> *And Cornelius said, Four days ago I was fasting until this hour; and at the ninth hour I prayed in my house, and, behold, a man stood before me in bright clothing, And said, Cornelius, thy prayer is heard, and thine alms are had in remembrance in the sight of God. Send therefore to Joppa, and call hither Simon, whose surname is Peter; he is lodged in the house of one Simon a tanner by the sea side: who, when he cometh, shall speak unto thee. Immediately therefore I sent to thee; and thou hast well done that thou art come. Now therefore are we all here present before God, to hear all things that are commanded thee of God. (Acts 10:30-33)*

Notice the word "commanded." What Peter was going to present to them are things that would be necessary for their salvation. This was the whole reason for Peter's going to them. Peter first began by explaining that God is not a respecter of persons but God accepts those who fear Him and work righteousness *(Acts 10:34-35)*. The rooftop vision was now becoming very clear to Peter. Peter began to speak about Jesus in the ways that he did in Acts 2, 3, and 5, that the gospel is the death, burial, and resurrection *(Acts10:38-40)*, and that the Apostles were chosen as eyewitnesses of His resurrection, even to the point of eating and drinking with them after He rose again. This is absolute proof that Jesus had risen from the dead. It is possible that Peter told Cornelius' household these things. The reason for this was because of some false teaching during that time that said that Jesus was a disembodied spirit being (*Gnosticism/Docetism*). It is no doubt that the Jesus before His crucifixion and the Jesus after the resurrection was the same person, except for the change in appearance: He now had a glorified body. While Peter continued to preach to the people, something extraordinary happened.

The Holy Ghost Falls Upon Cornelius' Household

> *While Peter yet spake these words, the Holy Ghost fell on all them which heard the word. And they of the circumcision which believed were astonished, as many as came with Peter, because that on the Gentiles also was poured out the gift of the Holy Ghost. For they heard them speak with tongues, and magnify God. Then answered Peter, Can any man forbid water, that these should not be baptized, which have received the Holy Ghost as well as we? And he commanded them to be baptized in the name of the Lord. Then prayed they him to tarry certain days. (Acts 10:44-48)*

All of a sudden, just like on Pentecost Sunday, the Holy Ghost fell on all of them that heard the word because of their faith in the word being preached. This was also a sign from God that He had now accepted the Gentiles into the Kingdom. The Jewish brethren (*circumcision*) that came with Peter were astonished; they were amazed and even beside themselves because they realized the Gentiles had been accepted by God and that Jesus had poured out His Spirit on them. Peter may have had a little advance notice about this, but these Jewish brethren were not privy to that information. Horton remarks that it was hard for these Jewish believers to believe that Gentiles could be accepted by God without first becoming Jews (16). There could be no doubt because God had given the Holy Ghost to these Gentile believers.

The question is, "How did they know that they received the Holy Ghost?" What was the sign that they had? The answer is found in verse

46: "For they heard them speak with tongues, and magnify God." Notice that there was no wind or tongues of fire like on the first Pentecost outpouring. Peter didn't even lay his hands on them, but the Gentiles began speaking in other languages as they were filled with the Holy Ghost and that was how they knew. As Ben Witherington explains it:

> As is often the case for Luke, it is the audible phenomenon that accompanies the event that convinces the circumcised believers that the Holy Spirit had fallen on the audience. They heard them speaking in tongues and praising God. [17]

This event at Cornelius' house mirrors the event in the upper room in the beginning of Acts 2. Both events involved the infilling of the Holy Ghost upon the individuals with evidence. The evidence was the supernatural sign of speaking in tongues. Menzies and Menzies discuss speaking in tongues as a sign of Spirit birth:

> Whether from the lips of a Jew in Jerusalem [2:4-5, 17-20] or a gentile in Syria, the manifestation of tongues-speech marks the speaker as a member of the end-time prophetic community. [18]

You would think that after this great experience, Peter's job was finished, but not yet. The born-again experience as Jesus explained to Nicodemus in John 3:3-5 was a New Birth of the water (*baptism*) and the Spirit (*receiving the Holy Ghost*). That is why the scripture tells us that Peter *commanded* them to be baptized. He didn't suggest or recommend that they should be baptized, he *commanded* them to do so, and they were baptized that very day in the Name of Jesus Christ. Then Cornelius' household requested that Peter and his Jewish brethren remain with them for a few days.

Why was it so necessary that Cornelius and his household be baptized since they had received the Holy Ghost? The New Birth is just that. It is a birth of water and Spirit. You cannot leave any part of the birth out. If you do, the birth is not complete. We sometimes want to ask, "When are our sins remitted?" or "When are they forgiven?" We try to give an answer like, "Our sins are forgiven in repentance and remitted at baptism," but truly, they both happen as the New Birth is completed.

News of the Gentile Conversion

Word got around fast that Peter was preaching the word to a Gentile audience, and they had received the word of God *(Acts 11:1)*. And when Peter came to Jerusalem, the Jewish brethren there were contending with him; they were not happy that he went to a Gentile's home and stayed there a few days. "You entered the home of Gentiles and even ate with them!" *(Acts 11:3 NLT)*.

Peter then began to recount the story beginning with his roof top experience. He told his brethren that the Lord told him to go with Cornelius' men doubting nothing *(vs 12)*. When Peter arrived at Cornelius' house, the man showed them how an angel had appeared unto him. Cornelius said that the angel told him to find Peter. When Peter asked Cornelius why he called for him, notice his answer: "Who shall tell thee words, whereby thou and all thy house shall be saved" *(Acts 11:14)*. Then Peter explained that as he was speaking to them, the Holy Ghost fell on them just like in the upper room on Pentecost.

Then remembered I the word of the Lord, how that he said, John indeed baptized with water; but ye shall be baptized with the Holy Ghost. (Acts 11:16)

Final Thoughts

When I hear of men and women pointing people to other areas of scripture to show a new convert how to be saved while omitting these accounts in the Book of Acts or telling them to just "believe on the

Lord," it grieves me. We can go back to chapter 3 (*of this book*) to understand why it was so important for Cornelius' family to not only receive the Holy Ghost—evidenced by their speaking in other tongues—but also the necessity to be baptized in the Name of Jesus Christ. Peter told his Jewish brethren:

Forasmuch then as God gave them? (Gentiles) the like gift as he did unto us, who believed on the Lord Jesus Christ; what was I, that I could withstand God? (Acts 11:17)

This is what was commanded by Jesus in the Great Commission that He left to His Apostles. And it is the Great Commission that we must follow. As Peter continued to tell his story, he explained that as he began to speak, the Gentiles received the Holy Ghost. Ben Witherington writes:

The interesting thing about this quote is that when Jesus used it, it was addressed to his Jewish followers, but now Peter is applying it to the Gentiles. For Peter, the decisive factor was that God gave the same gift to them, the Holy Spirit, as he gave those in the upper room when they believed in the Lord Jesus Christ. Thus he compares what happened in a Gentile house in Caesarea to what happened in the upper room in Jerusalem. [19]

Peter's own words were that God gave the Gentiles the *like gift* as He gave the 120 on the first Pentecost Sunday, along with the thousands that day "who believed on the Lord Jesus Christ." This *like gift* is available to us today. As Stanley Horton writes:

Surely, in the midst of all the questioning and discussion about the Holy Spirit today, we need the same convincing evidence. We too can know that when we speak in tongues we have received an experience identical to the one described in Acts 2:4. [20]

Have you received the Holy Ghost since you believed? When you "received" the Holy Ghost, did you speak in tongues? If not, how do you know whether or not you have received it? You must be sure of your New Birth experience.

8

AN ABOUT-FACE

When God truly gets a hold of a person's life, He will so radically change that individual that he will make a complete 180 degree "About-face." I can remember a time when my wife had just brought our first-born son into the world. As mentioned in my introduction, we were Roman Catholics at the time, and we were preparing to have our son christened. My brother Ralph was supposed to be my son's godfather. Traditionally, the role of the godparent was to present the child at baptism and promise to take responsibility for the child's religious education in the event that the parents could not do so. However, he called two weeks before the event and told me he could not stand in as my son's godfather. He told me he had received the gift of the Holy Ghost just like the Apostles did on the Day of Pentecost. Because of his new understanding of salvation, he could not promise to raise our son according to the Catholic faith. My wife and I were astounded at this news. This didn't sound at all like Ralph.

Ralph had gotten himself into quite a bit of trouble when he was a teenager. He hung around in gangs drinking and taking drugs to get high. He would even put glue in a bag and breathe it in to get a buzz.

My brother also got in a lot of trouble in school. But besides all this, Ralph didn't believe in God. I would always try to convince him there was a God, but he would always argue and disagree with me. So, you could see why we were so amazed when Ralph had claimed that he had an experience with God. We had judged Ralph by his past and by his outward appearance, but only God knows the heart.

We had a big party with family and friends following the church ceremony and when my brother entered the back yard, my wife and I just looked at him and knew that something definitely had changed him. It was as though his face was glowing and his entire demeanor had changed. It was after the party, when everyone had gone home, that Ralph showed us the scriptures and relayed the experience he had to that of the Apostles on the Day of Pentecost. He said that he spoke in tongues when he received the Holy Ghost. He told us that we could receive this great Gift of God also.

This fascinated us. My wife and I were drawn to the truth and power of his words. It was then we decided that we too would do an "about-face."

Saul of Tarsus

The Apostle Paul may be the greatest Christian witness for Jesus Christ ever. He was a great man who started many churches all over the world in his day, preached many Gospel messages, and gave Jesus Christ his all, even to the point of suffering greatly for His name, and in the end giving his life for his Lord. However, Paul was not always a great Christian preacher. In fact, as Saul of Tarsus, he hated the church and tried to destroy it. This chapter will deal with Saul's life before and after his conversion to Christianity.

The first time we hear of Saul of Tarsus he was standing by and watching as some Hebrew men stoned Stephen because they thought he had blasphemed God. Saul of Tarsus, who was by no means an innocent spectator, was consenting to or approving of the death of Stephen. The witnesses who by law were required to throw the first stones, laid their cloaks at the feet of Saul. He watched as Stephen, a man full of faith and Godly wisdom, drew his last breaths. He was an eyewitness to all that was done, including hearing the dying words of Stephen. Stephen's words mirrored the words of Jesus on the cross as he said, "Lord, lay not this sin to their charge." He died saying, "Lord Jesus, receive my spirit" *(Acts 7:60)*. We can only wonder how Stephen's death may have affected the soon to be Apostle Paul. This may have affected Paul to later desire the same things that he saw in Stephen when he wrote to the Philippians:

That I may know him (Jesus), and the power of his resurrection, and the fellowship of his sufferings, being made conformable unto his death; (Philippians 3:10)

The scripture says that these men laid their clothes at Saul's feet as they stoned Stephen.

And cast him out of the city, and stoned him: and the witnesses laid down their clothes at a young man's feet, whose name was Saul. (Acts 7:58)

What did this laying of the clothes at Saul's feet mean? Darrell Bock in his commentary on Acts has this explanation:

Luke introduces the hero of the second half of Acts by noting that he observes and shares in the persecution and rejection of Christians. He is an eyewitness to the nature of the dispute between many Jews in Jerusalem and the new community (Acts 22:20). Acts 8:1a notes that Saul approved of what was happening to Stephen, something Luke would have known as a companion of Paul. [1]

Acts 8:1 says, "And Saul was consenting unto his death." This means he approved of it. Dean Pinter says this of Saul's approving of Stephen's death:

> *This is a detail about the inner intent of Saul, one that he will make later himself in his own words (cf. 22:20). Luke could only have known about this inner attitude firsthand from Paul.* [2]

So, it appears that Saul was in agreement to the execution of Stephen and that it may have had a profound effect on the life and memory of Saul, for we hear him remembering his actions in Acts 22:20 as he spoke to the Lord:

> *And I said, Lord, they know that I imprisoned and beat in every synagogue them that believed on thee: And when the blood of thy martyr Stephen was shed, I also was standing by, and consenting unto his death, and kept the raiment of them that slew him. (Acts 22:19-20)*

Why Did Saul Hate the Christian Faith?

Saul was born in Tarsus, a city in Cilicia. "Saul of Tarsus" was his Jewish name. "Paul" was his Christian name, but Saul of Tarsus was a great Jewish leader.

> *He studied under Gamaliel who was the grandson of Hillel, a great Jewish scholar born in Babylon. He studied in Tarsus, which was the intellectual center of the world at that time. He believed that Jesus was a false Messiah. He despised Christ, and he would get permission to go from city to city to city to have the Christians arrested. He would cast his vote for their death. He despised the Christians because he thought they were propagating a false Messiah in Jesus Christ.* [3]

J.R. Miller had this to say about the reason Saul was so zealous against Christ:

> *He was a loyal Jew, and Jesus had been crucified by the rulers of his people as a blasphemer. In this hatred of the rulers of his nation to Jesus, Saul sympa-*

thized. That such a man should claim to be the Messiah foretold by the prophets, appeared to Saul proof that He was an impostor. According to Saul's thought, Jesus had fulfilled none of the Jewish expectations regarding the Messiah: He had established no kingdom; He had wrought no deliverance for His people. Thinking of Jesus in this way, Saul readily conceived that He was an impostor and that belief in Him as the Messiah was heresy, which he as a true Jew was bound to do all he could to stamp out. Saul was conscientious in his opinions concerning Jesus, and in his work as a persecutor. [4]

About that time a great persecution began and the Christians, except for the apostles, were scattered throughout Judea and Samaria. The scripture describes the intense desire of Saul to destroy this newfound faith in Jesus. "As for Saul, he made havock of the church, entering into every house, and haling men and women committed them to prison" *(Acts 8:3)*. Darrell Bock says:

It may well be, however, that this significant event such as Stephen's speech and death lead Saul to see a need to act against this vocal but lesser-known part of the church. He may sense that things are becoming serious, as Jews of all kinds are responding to the gospel and speaking up for Jesus while challenging Israel's need to come to faith. [5]

Saul was not only determined to arrest Christians in and around Jerusalem, but he attempted to widen his net to Damascus. This shows how intense and how hostile the attitude of Saul was against these believers.

And Saul, yet breathing out threatenings and slaughter against the disciples of the Lord, went unto the high priest, And desired of him letters to Damascus to the synagogues, that if he found any of this way, whether they were men or women, he might bring them bound unto Jerusalem. (Acts 9:1-2)

Later in his epistles Paul explains his zeal for God and why he persecuted the church:

> *For ye have heard of my conversation in time past in the Jews' religion, how that beyond measure I persecuted the church of God, and wasted it: And profited in the Jews' religion above many my equals in mine own nation, being more exceedingly zealous of the traditions of my fathers. (Galatians 1:13-14)*

> *Concerning zeal, persecuting the church; touching the righteousness which is in the law, blameless. (Philippians 3:6)*

> *And I persecuted this way unto the death, binding and delivering into prisons both men and women. (Acts 22:4)*

When he stood before King Agrippa in Acts 26, he said:

> *I verily thought with myself, that I ought to do many things contrary to the name of Jesus of Nazareth. Which thing I also did in Jerusalem: and many of the saints did I shut up in prison, having received authority from the chief priests; and when they were put to death, I gave my voice against them. And I punished them oft in every synagogue, and compelled them to blaspheme; and being exceedingly mad against them, I persecuted them even unto strange cities. (Acts 26:9-11)*

Such was the involvement of Saul in trying to round up all those who believed in Jesus Christ. Little did he know at that time, that soon he would be making an about-face as far as his faith was concerned. He would be as devout and zealous for Jesus Christ after his conversion as he was against the church before his conversion.

On the Road to Damascus

And as he journeyed, he came near Damascus: and suddenly there shined round about him a light from heaven: And he fell to the earth, and heard a voice saying unto him, Saul, Saul, why persecutest thou me? And he said, Who art thou, Lord? And the Lord said, I am Jesus whom thou persecutest: it is hard for thee to kick against the pricks. And he trembling and astonished said, Lord, what wilt thou have me to do? And the Lord said unto him, Arise, and go into the city, and it shall be told thee what thou must do. (Acts 9:3-6)

Saul of Tarsus had a life-altering experience on the way to Damascus. It is there that Jesus called out to him, asking him why he continually persecuted Him. Dean Pinter writes:

For those of us familiar only with English tenses (i.e., past, present, future), where the emphasis is on "time," it is important to know that in Greek the present tense emphasizes more the kind of action than the time when the action occurs. That is, Saul is persecuting "me" in an ongoing and continuous manner. [6]

The events unfolded as follows. As Saul was about to enter the city a great light from heaven suddenly shone like lightening all around him. Stanley Horton explains:

Saul, who is probably walking, recognized the light as beyond the ordinary, or supernatural, so fell face down to the ground, prostrating himself (as Orientals did to show humility, respect, and, sometimes, worship). [7]

Saul was about to enter Damascus, evidently continuing his persecution of the Christians, when all of a sudden, Jesus confronts him. Jesus was evidently taking Saul's persecution of the church as a personal affront against Himself. Notice His words, "Why are you persecuting me?" Saul answers with a question of his own, "Who are you, Lord?" This is not just a polite address. Saul was a Jew, so when he used the title Lord, he knew he was speaking of the One True God, Yahweh, for Saul knew no other God but One. How surprised he must have been when the voice answered back, "I am Jesus, whom you are persecuting." In persecuting the Church, Saul was persecuting Christ Himself. Saul was no longer the self-confident, self-assured person he was before, but now, he was trembling and asked Jesus, "What will you have me to do?" Jesus answered that Saul should go into the city, and there he would be told what he must do.

> *And the men which journeyed with him stood speechless, hearing a voice, but seeing no man. And Saul arose from the earth; and when his eyes were opened, he saw no man: but they led him by the hand, and brought him into Damascus. And he was three days without sight, and neither did eat nor drink. (Acts 9:7-9)*

Apparently only Saul saw the risen Jesus. His companions saw a light and heard a voice but didn't see anyone. When Saul opened his eyes, he was unable to see, and so he had to be led about by the hand until he was led into the city of Damascus. He was there three days, and he did not have anything to eat or drink during that time.

We don't know what was upon Saul's mind as he spent those three days in darkness, but he must have been thinking about his experience with Jesus. If Jesus was the Lord, then Saul would have to make an about-face as far as his thinking about Him. He no longer could be a false Messiah but He must be the true Messiah, His Lord, His God! Also, he must now become a part of the church he was formerly persecuting: the body of true believers. According to Dean Pinter:

> *This was not the arrival to Damascus that he anticipated. The Lord will shortly commission Saul to take the light of the gospel to the nations, but first Saul must sit it in darkness for three days. He must be converted from his condition of embodying Israel's blind resistance to the straightway of God.* [8]

Not only did Saul come face-to-face with Jesus, but his entire world, in that moment, was forever changed. Tony Merida says:

Saul's worldview got demolished. A new one was about to take its place. Jesus humbled this arrogant and violent man, turning the terrorist into a soon to be evangelist. The self-righteous persecutor is about to become the Christ centered apostle. [9]

Saul's "About-face"

And there was a certain disciple at Damascus, named Ananias; and to him said the Lord in a vision, Ananias. And he said, Behold, I am here, Lord. And the Lord said unto him, Arise, and go into the street which is called Straight, and inquire in the house of Judas for one called Saul, of Tarsus: for, behold, he prayeth, And hath seen in a vision a man named Ananias coming in, and putting his hand on him, that he might receive his sight. Then Ananias answered, Lord, I have heard by many of this man, how much evil he hath done to thy saints at Jerusalem: And here he hath authority from the chief priests to bind all that call on thy name. But the Lord said unto him, Go thy way: for he is a chosen vessel unto me, to bear my name before the Gentiles, and kings, and the children of Israel: For I will shew him how great things he must suffer for my name's sake. (Acts 9:10-16)

Ananias was called a disciple at Damascus and the Lord called to him in a vision to go and put his hands on a man called Saul who is in the house of Judas in the street called Straight. This Ananias was not an apostle, nor was it said that he was an officer or a deacon of the church. Ananias seemed to be just an ordinary believer who the Lord chose to use. Ananias objected at first. He told the Lord of the troubles this Saul had caused to many of the saints at Jerusalem. This was not an unreasonable request by Ananias, especially since he had heard of all the problems Saul had caused in the church at Jerusalem and what he planned to do in Damascus. But God told him that Saul was a chosen vessel of His and that he would suffer many things for Jesus' name's sake. Although Ananias originally protested, he humbled himself before the Lord and willingly obeyed.

> *And Ananias went his way, and entered into the house; and putting his hands on him said, Brother Saul, the Lord, even Jesus, that appeared unto thee in the way as thou camest, hath sent me, that thou mightest receive thy sight, and be filled with the Holy Ghost. And immediately there fell from his eyes as it had been scales: and he received sight forthwith, and arose, and was baptized. And when he had received meat, he was strengthened. Then was Saul certain days with the disciples which were at Damascus. (Acts 9:17-19)*

As Ananias entered the house and saw Saul, the first thing he did was lay his hands on him. He then called him, "Brother Saul." This must have been comforting to Saul in a sense, because he didn't know anybody, and this greeting showed that he had already entered into the fellowship of the saints. Ananias also confirmed that it was the Lord Jesus who met him on the way. Then Ananias explained that Jesus had sent him so that he could receive the Holy Ghost and receive his sight back. And when Ananias prayed for Him, Saul received his sight and was baptized in the name of Jesus Christ. How do we know that he was buried with Christ in baptism? Acts 22:12-16 tells us of his baptismal experience:

> *And one Ananias, a devout man according to the law, having a good report of all the Jews which dwelt there, Came unto me, and stood, and said unto me, Brother Saul, receive thy sight. And the same hour I looked up upon him. And he said, The God of our fathers hath chosen thee, that thou shouldest know his will, and see that Just One, and shouldest hear the voice of his mouth. For thou shalt be his witness unto all men of what thou hast seen and heard. And now why tarriest thou? arise, and be baptized, and wash away thy sins, calling on the name of the Lord. (Acts 22:12-16)*

> When Ananias spoke to Saul, he told him that he would be filled with the Holy Ghost. Did this happen at this time? Some commentators say that there is no record that he was filled with the Spirit at this time, though they say that they have no reason to doubt that this happened. [10]

Ananias told Saul that God had sent him so that he would be filled with the Spirit. So even though the scripture doesn't record the actual infilling of Saul, we know that the scripture states that Ananias was sent to Saul for the sole purpose of restoring his sight and for Saul to be filled with the Holy Ghost (*Acts 9:17*). He was then baptized in the name of Jesus Christ for the remission of his sins, and this implies that he must also had repented.

There should be no question that he repented because how can one receive God's Holy Spirit unless that person has first repented of his sins? Didn't his baptism show that he had done so? Would Ananias have baptized him if he hadn't repented? Would God fill a human temple that has not been cleansed of sin? It is obvious that Saul is converted at this point because without repentance you cannot receive the Holy Ghost. "I tell you, Nay: but, except ye repent, ye shall all likewise perish" *(Luke 13:3)*.

The laying on of hands, by the Apostles, is seen other places in the scriptures when praying for believers to receive the Holy Ghost. This will be discussed further in the next chapter. This is a part of New Testament salvation/conversion/New Birth. Mr. Horton indicates:

> *Saul's experience of being filled with the Holy Spirit was no different from what the believers experienced on the Day of Pentecost. We can be sure that Saul spoke in other tongues at that time, as they did in Acts 2:4.* [11]

In 1 Corinthians 14 the Apostle Paul addressed a misunderstanding and misuse of speaking in tongues, and also addressed regulating the use of the *Gift* of Tongues and the *Gift* of Interpretation of Tongues. The *Gift* of Tongues needs to be followed by the *Gift* of Interpretation of Tongues if the church is to be edified, which means to be built up, as "in the building of a house." [12]

> *No more than two or three should speak in tongues. They must speak one at a time, and someone must interpret what they say. But if no one is present who can interpret, they must be silent in your church meeting and speak in tongues to God privately.*
> *(1 Corinthians 14:27-28 NLT)*

In 1 Corinthians 14:15, it appears that Paul was saying that there were times when he both prayed and sang in the Spirit. This is different from the times that he spoke and prayed with his understanding. Then Paul outwardly said:

> *I thank my God, I speak with tongues more than ye all: Yet in the church I had rather speak five words with my understanding, that by my voice I might teach others also, than ten thousand words in an unknown tongue.*
> *(1 Corinthians 14:18-19)*

Usually verse 19 causes many opposed to speaking in tongues to remark that Paul is saying that tongues are not so important. But is that what he was really saying? He said that he spoke in tongues more than anyone else in the Corinthian Church; he also said that he would rather speak five words with his understanding than ten-thousand words in an unknown tongue. Why did he say that? He said this because he was teaching them how to properly operate in the Gifts of Tongues and the Interpretation of Tongues. Unless there is an interpreter present to interpret the message of the tongues, words would be unintelligible to those listening. The whole discourse was teaching the Corinthians that in all the speaking in tongues they must make sure that the church is being edified. Otherwise, the person doing the speaking should speak only to himself and to God (*1 Corinthians 14:27-28*).

From 1 Corinthians 14:18, we learn that Paul did speak in other tongues. When did he receive this ability? The answer is simple: when he first received the Holy Ghost. This was most likely at the same time when he was baptized in Jesus Name. So, we see again that what happened on Pentecost Sunday is being rehearsed over again, but not necessarily in the exact same manner. And the scripture says that Saul, "straightway," which means "immediately, forth with, as soon as," began to preach Christ [13]. And he preached about Christ with the same passion and fervency in which he tried in the past to destroy Christ. Now the hunter became the hunted!

> And straightway he preached Christ in the synagogues, that he is the Son of God. But all that heard him were amazed, and said; Is not this he that destroyed them which called on this name in Jerusalem, and came hither for that intent, that he might bring them bound unto the chief priests? But Saul increased the more in strength, and confounded the Jews which dwelt at Damascus, proving that this is very Christ. And after that many days were fulfilled, the Jews took counsel to kill him: (Acts 9:20-23)

Paul Preaching to Disciples at Ephesus

> And it came to pass, that, while Apollos was at Corinth, Paul having passed through the upper coasts came to Ephesus: and finding certain disciples, He said unto them, Have ye received the Holy Ghost since ye believed? And they said unto him, We have not so much as heard whether there be any Holy Ghost. (Acts 19:1-2)

In Paul's second missionary journey, the Apostle Paul went to Ephesus but stayed only a short time because he wanted to be back in Jerusalem for a certain feast. He did promise that he would return. On his third journey, he did spend about three years there. Acts 19 verse1 tells us that Paul came to the coast of Ephesus and found certain disciples there. Paul asks them the question, "Have ye received the Holy Ghost since ye believed?" Their answer was that they hadn't heard that there was any Holy Ghost *(v2)*. This was a group that was not aware of the Pentecostal outpouring of the Holy Ghost. I like what was said in the New Application Bible Commentary on Acts 19:2:

> *What is significant is that Paul specifically asked them whether they received the Holy Ghost when they believed (19:2). This suggests that people can really know when they receive the Holy Spirit. The response of these disciples was that they had not even heard that there was a Holy Spirit.* [14]

How can a person be certain that they have received the Holy Ghost? Answer: they will speak in an unknown tongue. The Apostle Paul continues to interrogate these certain disciples:

> *And he said unto them, Unto what then were ye baptized? And they said, Unto John's baptism. Then said Paul, John verily baptized with the baptism of repentance, saying unto the people, that they should believe on him which should come after him, that is, on Christ Jesus. When they heard this, they were baptized in the name of the Lord Jesus. And when Paul had laid his hands upon them, the Holy Ghost came on them; and they spake with tongues and prophesied. And all the men were about twelve. (Acts 19:3-7)*

Paul found out that these disciples had only been baptized unto John's baptism. Paul led them to believe on the One that John had been pointing his disciples to, that is on Jesus Christ. When they heard Paul say this, they were baptized in the Name of Jesus Christ, that Only Name given under heaven whereby we must be saved (*Acts 4:12*). But Paul didn't stop there. The scripture says that he laid his hands on them and the Holy Ghost came on them and they spoke with tongues and prophesied. This is just another place that looks back to Pentecost Sunday to see the response to the Gospel. Dean Pinter says it well in his commentary on Acts 19:1-7:

> *Descriptions of audible experience of tongues (and prophesy) occur elsewhere in Acts only two other times (2: 4 and 10: 46). There is no reason to suggest, however, that this was an uncommon experience elsewhere in the early church (e.g., Gal 3:5;4:6), including Paul's own life (see 1 Cor 14). It should be noted, however, that the specific mention of the manifestation of speaking in tongues occurs at significant junctures in the overall narrative. In each of these instances, a new and important work of the spirit is exhibited: (1) when the Jews received the Spirit on Pentecost (Acts 2:4); (2) when the first gentiles, Cornelius and his household, received the Spirit in Cesarea: (10:46); And now, (3) when this unnamed band of disciples receive the Spirit and in the strategic city of Ephesus.* [15]

The Apostle Paul employed a great practice that I think would be great if we would adopt. He noticed that the disciples of John did not have a full experience and had not received the Holy Ghost or been baptized in Jesus' name. Yet Paul does not try to take away from these disciples what they've already experienced but he begins to add on to their belief by pointing them to the one whom John preached about when he baptized people. When they understood that Jesus was the one John pointed to, they gladly desired to be baptized in the Name of Jesus Christ and then Paul was able to lay hands on them and by faith they received the power of the Holy Ghost, spoke in tongues and prophesied. We should always try to add to a person's experience, not take away from it. Even though some Christians have not understood the Acts 2:38 message, that does not mean that they have no relationship with God. We need to *add* to their experience and knowledge.

Why Did God Choose Tongues as a Sign that Someone has Received the Holy Ghost?

1. God is sovereign and He can do as He pleases. God does not answer to us, but we to him. God could have chosen anything He desired to as a sign that someone has received

the Gift of the Holy Ghost, but He has chosen tongues as the sign.
2. Speaking in tongues is the universal evidence of receiving the Holy Ghost. It applies to all, regardless of race, culture, educational level, or financial status. Not all people will react the same emotionally or physically when filled with the Holy Ghost. However, everyone who receives the Spirit will speak in tongues as the Spirit gives the utterance.
3. Speaking in tongues is evidence of a supernatural work on the inside. Jesus once said:

In the last day, that great day of the feast, Jesus stood and cried, saying, If any man thirst, let him come unto me, and drink. He that believeth on me, as the scripture hath said, out of his belly shall flow rivers of living water. (But this spake he of the Spirit, which they that believe on him should receive: for the Holy Ghost was not yet given; because that Jesus was not yet glorified.) (John 7:37-39) When someone receives the Holy Ghost, some say it feels like rivers of living water are flowing out of their innermost being. This was my wife's experience. Jesus explained this as speaking of the Spirit which they which believe on Him should receive.

1. According to the Apostle James, although it is a small member of the body, the tongue is able to control, direct, and defile the whole body.

Behold, how great a matter a little fire kindleth! And the tongue is a fire, a world of iniquity: so is the tongue among our members, that it defileth the whole body, and setteth on fire the course of nature; and it is set on fire of hell. (James 3:6)

2. Before an individual can receive the Holy Ghost, he or she must surrender his or her whole being to God. The last member of the human body to be surrendered to God is the tongue. Only God can

tame the tongue. "But the tongue can no man tame; it is an unruly evil, full of deadly poison." *(James 3:8)*. Jesus said:

A good man out of the good treasure of his heart bringeth forth that which is good; and an evil man out of the evil treasure of his heart bringeth forth that which is evil: for of the abundance of the heart his mouth speaketh. (Luke 6:45)

3. Before a person receives the Holy Ghost, they must repent of their sins and be willing to be baptized in Jesus Name. Once a person repents, God forgives their sins and now the heart is pure and swept clean. At that moment, when someone is filled with the Holy Ghost, God fills their being and from out of the abundance of a pure and clean heart the mouth speaks forth as God gives the utterance.

Final Thoughts

God is still working in the hearts of men and women who will dare to believe that they can receive the Gift of the Holy Ghost, and speak in unknown tongues as the Spirit of God gives them the utterance. I too have had this experience and have seen firsthand many people receive it. Because it is a supernatural happening many people are afraid of receiving the Holy Ghost, but it's not something in which to be fearful. Rather it is something to be desired.

People may have a relationship with God that have never spoken in tongues, but if there is more to add to your experience with our Great Supernatural Father, why wouldn't you want it? God poured out His Spirit on the first Pentecost Sunday, and He has been doing so ever since. People are repenting of their sins, being baptized in the Name of Jesus Christ for the forgiveness of their sins, and they are receiving the Gift of the Holy Ghost speaking in other tongues as the Spirit of God gives them the utterance to do so. Every day people are making an "About-face." Will you?

9
THE GOSPEL TO SAMARIA

And Saul was consenting unto his death. And at that time there was a great persecution against the church which was at Jerusalem; and they were all scattered abroad throughout the regions of Judaea and Samaria, except the apostles. And devout men carried Stephen to his burial, and made great lamentation over him. As for Saul, he made havock of the church, entering into every house, and haling men and women committed them to prison. (Acts 8:1-3)

Since this subject was dealt with in Chapter 8, we will not deal with it again here except to say that after Stephen's death a great persecution arose against the Church. It seems that Stephen's death was the spark that fueled this persecution and it was intense enough that the Christians in Jerusalem, except the apostles, were scattered throughout the regions of Judea and Samaria. Acts 11:19 tells us that they travelled as far as Phenice, Cyprus, and Antioch, preaching the Word to the Jews only. But according to Horton:

Saul became more and more furious, more violent in his persecution. In fact, he 'made havoc of the Church' (8:3) Literally he kept on ravaging and devastating it. Entering house after house, he dragged out men and women and handed them over to be put into prison. Then, as we learn later, when they were brought to trial he cast his vote to have them killed (Acts 22:4; 26:10).* [1]

We often think that God should deliver us out of all trouble all the time. If He doesn't deliver us, we question why He didn't. But when we look at Stephen's death, we see that he was serving God, leading a good life, preaching the gospel, and standing for the truth against a mob ready to stone him, and God didn't deliver him. Ajith Fernando in the NIV Application Commentary makes a great point about Christian suffering. He tells us that Stephen's experience with death is given here in Acts Chapter 8 to help us face suffering.

Steven's anointing with the Spirit's fullness took the form of a vision of God's glory and of the exalted Christ in his role as advocate and heaven. Through it Stephen received strength to face his painful ordeal triumphantly. On many occasions in Acts when God's servants suffered for the gospel, God revealed himself in some recognizable way that gave them the courage to go on (4: 31; 18: 9; 23:11; 27: 23-24). We can conclude that God, knowing how much we can endure, gives us His strength in our times of need, which boosts our spirits and spurs us on to obedience, even to obedience leading to death. In a similar way God fulfilled this promise in the life of Paul when no relief from suffering came to him: "My grace is sufficient for you, for my power is made perfect in weakness." (2 Corinthians 12: 9) [2]

God did not deliver many of the 1st Century Christians that lost their lives in the Colosseum or those who died by crucifixion in Nero's courtyard. And He may not deliver us. However, the persecution did not stop the spread of the Gospel. The scripture records: "Therefore they that were scattered abroad went everywhere preaching the word" (Acts 8:4).

The one great take away from all this is that the Gospel was not hindered. Those who were scattered went about preaching the word of God, the Gospel of Jesus Christ, everywhere they went. "Persecution does to the church what the wind does to seed; it scatters it. The believers were God's seed and the persecution was used by God to plant them in new soil so they could bear fruit." [3]

The Gospel is Preached in Samaria

This is what Jesus said in Acts 1:8, that after they received the Holy Ghost, they would be filled with power to be witnesses unto Him in Jerusalem, Judea, Samaria and to the uttermost parts of the world. The greater part of Acts Chapter 8 deals with the Gospel being preached in Samaria by Philip. Samaria was the capital of the northern kingdom of Israel.

> *In 726–722 BC, the new king of Assyria, Shalmaneser V, invaded the land and besieged the city of Samaria. After an assault of three years, the city fell and much of its population was taken into captivity and deported.*[4]

The Jews despised the Samaritans, mainly because the people of the northern kingdom of Israel intermarried with the descendants of the pagan tribes of the Assyrians. The Jews may have hated them worse than the Gentiles. But during Jesus' ministry, there were times when He reached out to, or made good examples of the Samaritans in His teachings. In Luke Chapter 10, we read the parable of the good Samaritan, the man who took care of the Jew who fell into the hands of robbers. Jesus taught that his Jewish brothers left him for dead, but this hated Samaritan came to his rescue. When Jesus healed the 10 lepers in Luke Chapter 17, the only one who returned to give thanks to God was a Samaritan. In one of the more famous accounts in John's Gospel, Jesus is conversing with a woman of Samaria at a well in Chapter 4. In fact, Jesus stayed two days with the people in Samaria simply because they believed in Him and desired that He would stay with them. According to Acts 1:8, Samaria was next to receive the Gospel.

> *Then Philip went down to the city of Samaria, and preached Christ unto them. And the people with one accord gave heed unto those things which Philip spake, hearing and seeing the miracles which he did. For unclean spirits, crying with loud voice, came out of many that were possessed with them: and many taken with palsies, and that were lame, were healed. And there was great joy in that city. (Acts 8:5-8)*

When Philip got to Samaria "he preached Christ unto them" *(Acts 8:5)*. The result was that the Samaritans paid attention to Philip's preaching because they heard and saw the miracles he was performing *(Acts 8:6)*. The witnesses saw many diverse miracles including healings of those that were lame and of those that had palsies. They also witnessed the casting out of evil spirits. The scripture records that there was great joy in the city *(Acts 8:8)*. Here it seems that the miraculous was greatly responsible for the Samaritans believing the Gospel.

Simon the Sorcerer

> *But there was a certain man, called Simon, which before time in the same city used sorcery, and bewitched the people of Samaria, giving out that himself was some great one: To whom they all gave heed, from the least to the greatest, saying, This man is the great power of God. And to him they had regard, because that of long time he had bewitched them with sorceries. (Acts 8:9-11)*

There was a man named Simon, who was a sorcerer practicing magic in the city. In fact, some in the city were astonished at the things he did even claiming that he was someone great saying that "this man was the power of God" *(Acts 8:10)*. Simon was a sorcerer who was well known outside the NT in early Christianity.

> *Justin Martyr wrote about Simon Magnus coming to Rome during the reign of Claudius. According to Justin, Simon had a significant following amongst Samaritans living in Rome who honored him as a 'god' and revered him with an altar and statue dedicated to him... Further, Irenaeus, a second century apologist, regarded Simon Magnus as a forerunner of the gnostic heresy. These stories are later developments from the description in Acts. Still, what is clear is that there was a Simon from Samaria who had a negative impact on the early church that originated from his first encounter with Christianity through Phillip.* [5]

Apparently, Simon had bewitched the people for some time and they were amazed at the magical things he did. But as so often is the case with the devil's deceptive tricks, it leaves the hearts of people unfulfilled. They may have been amazed at his magic, but his magic couldn't do what the gospel can. Bible scholars are divided on whether or not Simon's faith was indeed genuine. Some believe that he was sincere and continued to follow Philip. Still another counts "his faith sincere but confused [6]." Whatever may have been the case then, Peter later rebukes Simon for thinking that the gift of God could be purchased with money.

Philip Preaches Christ unto Them

> *But when they believed Philip preaching the things concerning the kingdom of God, and the name of Jesus Christ, they were baptized, both men and women. (Acts 8:12)*

Simon may have held the interest of the people for a time but when the real deal came to town the people's interest in Simon faded and they began to follow Philip. The scripture says that Philip preached Christ unto them. That's really all we have to do to reach people for God. It's the simplicity of the gospel that opens the eyes of those who have a desire to serve Jesus Christ. And all the people in one accord paid attention to the words of Philip and they saw the miracles he did, even casting out unclean spirits. Many were healed of their infirmities and there was great joy in the city. As Philip preached the things that pertain unto the Kingdom of God and the Name of Jesus Christ, the people were baptized, both men and women, in the wonderful Name of Jesus Christ.

The mention of believing in the name of Jesus refers to responding to His power and occurs several times in Acts (2: 38; 3: 6; 4: 8-10; 8: 12; 10: 48; 16: 18). The Kingdom was one of Jesus's favorite topics in his teaching. This is one of eight uses of the term 'kingdom' in Acts but is the first since Jesus spoke to the disciples about it during His 40 days with them after the resurrection. [7]

Then Simon himself believed also: and when he was baptized, he continued with Philip, and wondered, beholding the miracles and signs which were done. (Acts 8:13)

The good news of the Kingdom was the preaching of the Gospel of Jesus Christ. J. Dwight Pentecost says:

This reveals that the Kingdom of God as it is used here is a reference to God's program in this present age of bringing men to himself through the preaching of the death and resurrection of Jesus Christ... Those who believed publicly identified themselves with Jesus Christ by baptism. [8]

The scripture even tells us that Simon also believed and was baptized and then he continued to follow Philip because he was amazed at the miracles and wonders done by the hand of Philip. Here was a man that was able to do a few of the devil's tricks but when he encountered a true man of God, he was amazed at the miracles because he could not do them.

Now when the apostles which were at Jerusalem heard that Samaria had received the word of God, they sent unto them Peter and John: Who, when they were come down, prayed for them, that they might receive the Holy Ghost: (For as yet he was fallen upon none of them: only they were baptized in the name of the Lord Jesus.). (Acts 8:14-16)

Now when word got back to Jerusalem that Samaria *(a great many of them)* had received the Word of God, Peter and John were sent unto them. Philip had been the instrumental one in preaching the Gospel, and many great things had happened. The Samaritans believed the words which Philip spoke and many of them had been healed and had seen many miraculous things. However, even though the Samaritans had believed and been baptized in the name of Jesus Christ, they had not yet received the gift of the Holy Ghost.

At this point we need to address a couple of questions. First, why were Peter and John sent for, probably by Philip, to come to Samaria? Secondly, how did Philip understand that none of the Samaritans had received the Holy Ghost, since most teachers and scholars today say that you receive it when you believe on the Lord or accept the Lord as your personal Savior? Philip had experienced receiving the Holy Ghost himself and he must have witnessed many others also receiving it while in Jerusalem before the persecution made him flee to Samaria. What was missing in the experience of the Samaritans?

Why did Peter and John come down to Samaria? Why didn't the Samaritans receive the Holy Ghost before Peter and John came? How did Philip know that the Samaritans had not received the Holy Ghost? Apparently, Peter and John, who were considered leaders and spokesmen in the early church, may have gone down to Samaria to verify what had taken place through the ministry of Philip. They found that the Samaritans had believed and had been baptized in water in the name of Jesus Christ, but they had not yet received the gift of the Holy Ghost as all those who did on the Day of Pentecost. Stanley Horton states:

> *The gospel had gotten beyond its first ethnic and geographic hurdle. So, the apostles sent Peter and John to Samaria (with a message and a purpose) to find out the facts and encourage the new believers.* [9]

Simply put, there was still work to do in Samaria. From Jesus at the well talking to the woman in John 4 to Philip arriving in a city of Samaria to preach the Word of God in Acts 8, Samaria was primed for revival. Just like in today's times, spreading the Gospel is not just a one-man job. Philip needed reinforcements, and that is exactly what happened when Peter and John arrived. As Dean Pinter explains:

> *What Luke seems to indicate is that in this first reception of the good news outside Jerusalem, the apostles' presence is required to complete the process. Since the Samaritan mission is such a radical first step, all the parties involved need a divine affirmation of the legitimacy of this mission. This may be why outward expressions of the Spirit occur only after the coming of Peter and John and the laying on of their hands.* [10]

Philip not only needed Peter and John's help in Samaria, but the Samaritans needed them there too. They needed to see firsthand witnesses to this powerful Gospel message. Tony Merida gives his thoughts:

> *The Spirit is withheld until the apostles could verify the gospel work. In this unique case of the gospel's first moving beyond Jerusalem, the Lord sovereignly waited to give any manifestation of the Spirit until the apostles could be there to witness it. That way they would see and could testify that the Samaritans received the same Holy Spirit given to the Christians in Jerusalem. In this way there could be no question that the gospel was for the nations and that the Jews and Samaritans, once bitter enemies, were now brothers and sisters and members of the same household of God because of their shared faith.* [11]

Receiving the Holy Ghost is a unique experience outside of repentance and water baptism. All three are part of the new birth process. There was great work happening in Samaria, but the work was incomplete without the infilling of the Spirit. David Bernard says:

> *This incident reveals that the baptism of the Spirit is a definite experience not to be confused with and not necessarily accompanying miracles, great emotion, mental belief, repentance, or water baptism. When the apostles heard what was happening in Samaria, they sent Peter and John. When Peter and John prayed for the Samaritans and laid hands of them, they received the Holy Ghost (Acts 8:17). The Samaritans did not receive the Holy Ghost until Peter and John laid hands on them. Apparently they were not fully prepared earlier. They had 'believed Philip,' but evidently they had not committed themselves totally to Christ. When Peter and John arrived, prayed for them, and laid hands on them, their faith increased to the point of receiving the Spirit.* [12]

Now when Peter and John prayed for and laid hands on them, they received the Holy Ghost (*Acts 8:17*). How is it that now we are told that the Samaritans had received the Holy Ghost? How did Philip and the apostles know that the Samaritans had received the Holy Ghost? The answer is that they spoke in tongues just like the Christians in Jerusalem did when they received the Holy Ghost. There are some scholars and commentators that don't believe that speaking in tongues is the initial evidence that someone has received the Holy Spirit. How is that so?

When you look at what happened in Samaria and compare it to what happened at Pentecost (*Acts 2*) and what is written in Acts 10, 11, and 19, we have to admit that something very distinct happens to a person when they receive the Holy Spirit. There is an outward sign or evidence that this had taken place. This is how we can know for sure that we have received God's Holy Spirit.

As the Samaritans were receiving the Holy Spirit, Simon saw what was happening and wanted to buy the power, so that when he laid his hands on someone, they would receive the Holy Spirit (*Acts 8:19*).

Simon saw something very real happen. I have seen people react in many ways when they receive the Holy Spirit. Some will shout and dance about, some kneel with their face in their hands. Others will laugh out loud and others will just be still and cry. My mother, a dignified woman, stood and danced around a chair. People may react to the Spirit of God filling them in many ways, but the one thing that is always present is that they speak in tongues as the Spirit gives the utterance. That is stated plainly in Acts 2, 10, 11, and 19, and it is inferred in Acts 8 and other places throughout the book.

The Ethiopian Eunuch

There is a passage towards the end of Acts 8, where the Lord has a new work for His evangelist. The Lord takes Philip away from what's happening in Samaria and sends him south toward the desert of Gaza. Why would the Lord remove Philip from seeing the end of the work he started in Samaria? God saw a man with a hungry heart with no one to minister to him. So, Philip was called upon one more time:

> *And the angel of the Lord spake unto Philip, saying, Arise, and go toward the south unto the way that goeth down from Jerusalem unto Gaza, which is desert. And he arose and went: and, behold, a man of Ethiopia, an eunuch of great authority under Candace queen of the Ethiopians, who had the charge of all her treasure, and had come to Jerusalem for to worship Was returning, and sitting in his chariot read Esaias the prophet.* (Acts 8:26-28)

Philip obeyed the Lord and he met with the eunuch from Ethiopia, who was returning from worshipping the Lord in Jerusalem. We see here the true heart of Philip. Many Christians today would argue with God saying, "I started this work and I should be there until it is completed." This usually occurs because many today are too possessive of their ministries and the things they do for the Lord. In a sense, we want all the recognition, and sometimes we even want some of the glory. However, Philip did not argue with God when He sent him down to a desert place. Philip understood that God is the one who gets the glory, not us. Philip completely obeyed the Lord and went down to Gaza.

The Ethiopian eunuch was an important official who was in charge of all the treasury of Candace, who was the queen of the Ethiopians. Dean Pinter points out that Philip went from preaching in Samaria, who was a near neighbor, to meeting this Ethiopian eunuch, who is from Cush which would be considered as the "ends of the earth" [13]. This of course would be a fulfilment of Acts 1:8 where Jesus said that those filled with the Holy Ghost would be witnesses to those in Jerusalem, and in all Judaea, and in Samaria, and unto the uttermost parts of the earth.

> *Then the Spirit said unto Philip, Go near, and join thyself to this chariot. And Philip ran thither to him, and heard him read the prophet Esaias, and said, Understandest thou what thou readest? And he said, How can I, except some man should guide me? And he desired Philip that he would come up and sit with him. (Acts 8:29-31)*

Philip is again directed by the Lord to "join himself to this chariot." As he is running alongside the chariot, he heard the eunuch reading from the Prophet Isaiah. Philip asked him if he understood what he was reading. The eunuch replied, "How can I, except some man would guide me?" So, Philip sat up in the chariot with the eunuch. Verse 32 tells us that the Ethiopian eunuch was reading from Isaiah 53:7-8.

> *He was oppressed, and he was afflicted, yet he opened not his mouth: he is brought as a lamb to the slaughter, and as a sheep before her shearers is dumb, so he openeth not his mouth. He was taken from prison and from judgment: and who shall declare his generation? for he was cut off out of the land of the living: for the transgression of my people was he stricken. (Isaiah 53:7-8)*

The eunuch asked Philip, "I pray thee, of whom speaketh the prophet this? of himself, or of some other man?" (*v. 34*) The scripture then tells us that Philip began at this scripture and preached Jesus unto him. He preached the Gospel of the death, burial, and the resurrection of Jesus Christ (*He preached Jesus unto him Acts 8:35*). He must have also preached baptism to him, as he did to the Samaritans earlier in Chapter 8, because when they came to a body of water, the eunuch asked Philip, "See, here is water; what doth hinder me to be baptized?" Philip's answer was: "...If thou believest with all thine heart, thou mayest. And he answered and said, I believe that Jesus Christ is the Son of God" *(Acts 8:37).*

Some commentators question whether or not the Ethiopian eunuch was ready to be baptized. If Philip was consistent in his preaching, he would have told the Ethiopian about repentance before baptism. This passage doesn't mention repentance, but we see earlier in Acts and in the Gospels that repentance is necessary before anyone can come to God for it is a turning away from sin and turning to God (*Lk 24:47; Acts 2:38, 3:19,5:31,11:18, 20:21, 26:20*). In repentance we ask God to forgive our sins. In fact, Jesus Himself spoke of repentance:

1. *"I tell you, Nay: but, except ye repent, ye shall all likewise perish." (Luke 13:3)*
2. *"And that repentance and remission of sins should be preached in his name among all nations, beginning at Jerusalem." (Luke 24:47)*

If Philip was consistent in preaching Christ unto him, he would have certainly mentioned repentance and the remission of sins in the name of Jesus Christ. Stanley Horton says in his commentary:

But Philip only began at Isaiah 53. He went on to explain the gospel further, with its commands, promises, and call to repentance, as Peter did (Acts 2:38). He made it clear that without Jesus no one can properly understand the Old Testament Scriptures. [14]

Finally, the passage says that after the eunuch was baptized, the Lord caught Philip away and the eunuch saw him no more, and he went on his way rejoicing, possibly meaning that he was filled with the Holy Ghost.

Acts 16: Lydia

The sixteenth chapter of Acts introduces two new people who Paul encounters while he is in the region of Macedonia. One night Paul had a vision: a man from Macedonia appeared to him pleading with him to come over to Macedonia and help them. So, Paul immediately decided to leave for Macedonia (*vs 9-10*). After arriving in Philippi, Paul and Silas traveled a little way outside the city on the Sabbath and went down to a place where some women were praying, and he went to speak to them. One of the women was Lydia, who was a wealthy woman who had a business as a dealer in fine purple cloth and dye, which was very expensive. She was also a worshipper of God.

Dean Pinter tells us that Lydia was a woman of means since she was dealing with a high-end product in the expensive commodity of purple cloth. He also says that she was a woman committed to Yahweh God because she is mentioned in the scripture as a worshiper of God. [15]

> *As she listened to us, the Lord opened her heart,* **and she accepted what Paul was saying**. *She was baptized along with other members of her household, and she asked us to be her guests. (Acts 16:14-15 NLT; bold emphasis mine)*

God opened Lydia's heart so that she could hear and understand what Paul was telling her. What did Paul speak to Lydia about? Paul preached the gospel of Jesus Christ to her. How do we know that? The Bible says that "She and her whole household were baptized" (*vs 15*). The NLT Application Bible says for verse [15]:

Why was Lydia's household baptized after Lydia responded in faith to the Good News? Baptism was a public sign of identification with Jesus Christ and the Christian community. [16]

Whenever the gospel is preached there should be a response in faith by the hearer. When someone truly believes the truth, their faith should lead them to repent of their sins, be baptized in the name of Jesus Christ for the remission of sins and they shall receive the gift of the Holy Ghost *(Acts 2:38, 8:12-17, 10:44-48, 19:1-6)*. The scripture goes on to say:

> *And when she was baptized, and her household, she besought us, saying, If ye have judged me to be faithful to the Lord, come into my house, and abide there. And she constrained us. (Acts 16:15)*

> *She was baptized along with other members of her household, and she asked us to be her guests.* ***"If you agree that I am a true believer in the Lord,"*** *she said, "come and stay at my home." And she urged us until we agreed. (Acts 16:15 NLT; bold emphasis mine)*

Lydia tells Paul: "If you agree that I am a true believer in the Lord... come and stay at my home" *(vs 15)*. The only way Paul could accept her as a true believer is if she was born again into the Kingdom of God *(John 3:3-5)*. That would mean that she had repented of her sins, was baptized in the name of Jesus, and had received the gift of the Holy Ghost. Ben Witherington III explains in his commentary that Paul must have believed her conversion was genuine:

> *The proof of conversion is shown in her imploring Paul and his colleagues to come and stay at her home, 'if you have judged me to be faithful to the Lord.' This was a powerful rhetorical approach. To refuse hospitality was always a serious breach of etiquette in antiquity, but to do so in this case would in addition suggest that Paul and Luke and Silas and Timothy thought Lydia's conversion and faithfulness were less than genuine.* [17]

Paul preached only ONE gospel and he makes this very clear in the Book of Galatians.

> *But though we, or an angel from heaven, preach any other gospel unto you than that which we have preached unto you, let him be accursed. As we said before, so say I now again, If any man preach any other gospel unto you than that ye have received, let him be accursed. (Galatians 1:8-9)*

Paul was also very clear that no one taught him what to preach except Jesus Christ Himself.

> *Dear brothers and sisters, I want you to understand that the gospel message I preach is not based on mere human reasoning. I received my message from no human source, and no one taught me. Instead, I received it by direct revelation from Jesus Christ. (Galatians 1:11-12 NLT)*

> *But even before I was born, God chose me and called me by his marvelous grace. Then it pleased him to reveal his Son to me so that I would proclaim the Good News about Jesus to the Gentiles. When this happened, **I did not rush out to consult with any human being. Nor did I go up to Jerusalem to consult with those who were apostles before I was.** Instead, I went away into Arabia, and later I returned to the city of Damascus. **Then three years later I went to Jerusalem to get to know Peter, and I stayed with him for fifteen days.** The only other apostle I met at that time was James, the Lord's brother. I declare before God that what I am writing to you is not a lie. (Galatians 1:15-20 NLT; bold emphasis mine)*

> ***Then fourteen years later I went back to Jerusalem again**, this time with Barnabas; and Titus came along, too. I went there because God revealed to me that I should go. **While I was there I met privately with those considered to be leaders of the church and shared with them the message I had been preaching to the Gentiles. I wanted to make sure that we were in agreement, for fear that all my efforts had been***

wasted and I was running the race for nothing. *And they supported me and did not even demand that my companion Titus be circumcised, though he was a Gentile.* (Galatians 2:1-3 NLT; bold emphasis mine)

And the leaders of the church had nothing to add to what I was preaching. *(By the way, their reputation as great leaders made no difference to me, for God has no favorites.)* ⁷ ***Instead, they saw that God had given me the responsibility of preaching the gospel to the Gentiles, just as he had given Peter the responsibility of preaching to the Jews.*** ⁸ ***For the same God who worked through Peter as the apostle to the Jews also worked through me as the apostle to the Gentiles.*** (Galatians 2:6-10 NLT; bold emphasis mine)

Notice that when Paul started preaching the Good News, he didn't consult with any other human beings. In fact, he went into Arabia and then into the city of Damascus. He waited three years before consulting with the Apostle Peter, and he stayed with him for fifteen days. Why did Paul consult with Peter?

Paul wanted to make sure that he and the other Apostles were in complete agreement as to the content of their message. Why? Because Paul believed that there was and is only one Gospel message. He said that he wanted to be in agreement for fear that all his efforts had been wasted and that he was running the race for nothing (*Gal 2:2*). How could their message have been in agreement? It was because Jesus was the originator of the gospel message and the correct response to it. Jesus told the Apostles what to tell those that would ask the question, "What shall we do to be saved?" Just compare the Great Commission in all four Gospels to how Peter responded to their question, and you will see that they are the same. This was fully explained in Chapter 4: Peter's First Gospel Sermon.

I find the story of Paul meeting the disciples of John in Acts Chapter 19 very compelling. If Paul had not visited with Peter or any other apostle, how did he know what to say to those disciples of John? We may want to overlook what happened there, but it is very fascinating that Paul told that group of twelve men that they needed to do exactly what Peter told over three thousand people what to do on the Day of Pentecost. The reason that this is so fascinating is that both Peter and Paul received their instructions from the same person: Jesus Christ. Then if this is so, why do so many ministers fail to inform their congregations that this is what they must do to be saved? Hopefully the efforts of all our ministers today will not be wasted, and they are not running this race for nothing.

Acts Chapter 16: The Philippian Jailer

After staying with Lydia, Paul and Silas were going to a place of prayer when a female slave, who was demon possessed, began following them. This slave made a great deal of money for her owners. She was following Paul and Silas and saying that they were servants of the Most High God, and she kept this up for many days. After a while, Paul had enough, and he cast the evil spirit out of her. Of course, this meant that she would no longer be telling fortunes and this would cause her owners' money-making scheme to die.

Her owners were very angry, and they seized Paul and Silas and brought them before the authorities complaining that these men were teaching customs that were unlawful for them to receive as Romans. Paul and Silas were then beaten and cast into prison. The jailer was told to keep them safely. The jailer then put them into an inner prison and bound their feet in stocks. The scripture then says:

> *And at midnight Paul and Silas prayed, and sang praises unto God: and the prisoners heard them. And suddenly there was a great earthquake, so that the foundations of the prison were shaken: and immediately all the doors were opened, and every one's bands were loosed. (Acts 16:25-26)*

At midnight, as Paul and Silas worshipped God freely while being incarcerated, God caused a great earthquake to shake the foundations of the prison. Every prison door was opened, and all the prisoners' chains were loosed. You can imagine how that jailer must have felt after both hearing the worship and then experiencing this great earthquake. The jailer was about to kill himself when he heard Paul cry out: "Do thyself no harm: for we are all here" (*vs. 28*). What happened next was God-orchestrated:

> *Then he called for a light, and sprang in, and came trembling, and fell down before Paul and Silas, And brought them out, and said, Sirs, what must I do to be saved? And they said, Believe on the Lord Jesus Christ, and thou shalt be saved, and thy house. (Acts 16:29-31)*

This is where so many preachers, teachers, and writers of Christian books bring people when they want to know how to be saved. Of course, it seems it should be very clear. Paul was asked, "What must I do to be saved?" and he answered, "Believe on the Lord Jesus Christ, and thou shalt be saved, and thy house (v. 31)." Based on the numerous other accounts in Acts, Paul and Silas understood that believing on the Lord Jesus Christ required action. Just because the next events are not explicitly outlined in Scripture doesn't mean this is where the story ends. When this question was asked in Acts 2, the response is much more defined:

> *Now when they heard this, they were pricked in their heart, and said unto Peter and to the rest of the apostles,* **Men and brethren, what shall we do?**" *(Acts 2:37; bold emphasis mine)*

But this time the answer was:

> *Then Peter said unto them, Repent, and be baptized every one of you in the name of Jesus Christ for the remission of sins, and ye shall receive the gift of the Holy Ghost. For the promise is unto you, and to your children, and to all that are afar off, even as many as the Lord our God shall call. (Acts 2:38-29)*

When we examine Acts 10, we find that an angel tells Cornelius to find Peter. Here is why:

He lodgeth with one Simon a tanner, whose house is by the sea side: **he shall tell thee what thou oughtest to do.** *(Acts 10:6; bold emphasis mine)*

As we look further into Chapter 10, Peter goes with Cornelius' men and begins to preach Jesus Christ to them. Before Peter ever gets finished with his message, the Holy Ghost falls on all of those in Cornelius' household, and they spoke in tongues and were baptized in Jesus' name. In Acts 11, Peter goes on the defensive. He had to explain to his Jewish brethren why he went into a Gentile's home and stayed a few days. Here was Cornelius' servants answer when Peter asked them why they were looking for him:

And he shewed us how he had seen an angel in his house, which stood and said unto him, Send men to Joppa, and call for Simon, whose surname is Peter; **Who shall tell thee words, whereby thou and all thy house shall be saved.** *And as I began to speak, the Holy Ghost fell on them, as on us at the beginning. (Acts 11:13-15; bold emphasis mine)*

We also have Acts 10 and 11 as an answer to the question, "What must I do to be saved?" Even the Apostle Paul told disciples of John how to be saved:

Then said Paul, John verily baptized with the baptism of repentance, saying unto the people, that they should believe on him which should come after him, that is, on Christ Jesus. When they heard this, they were baptized in the name of the Lord Jesus. And when Paul had laid his hands upon them, the Holy Ghost came on them; and they spake with tongues, and prophesied. (Acts 19:4-6)

Turning our attention back to the jailer in Acts Chapter 16, was Paul telling the jailer to only believe? Let's look at the rest of that story:

> *And they spake unto him the word of the Lord, and to all that were in his house. And he took them the same hour of the night, and washed their stripes; and was baptized, he and all his, straightway. And when he had brought them into his house, he set meat before them, and rejoiced, believing in God with all his house. (Acts 16:32-34)*

Now I know that it is imperative to believe, and faith is necessary for salvation even though it is not mentioned in Acts 2, 10 and 11. However, verse 32 says that Paul spoke unto him the Word of the Lord. What could he possibly be telling him? Could it be the gospel? Obviously, it must be because sometime a while after twelve midnight Paul baptized his whole household. Then they went back to the house and ate, and they rejoiced.

Some may argue that the Bible does not explicitly say that either the eunuch, Lydia, or the jailer received the Holy Ghost. David Bernard writes the following in his book *The New Birth*:

> *Some claim that people in the Book of Acts were saved without receiving the Spirit. For example, the Bible does not explicitly record that the following received the Holy Spirit: the 5000 who believed after the healing of the lame man (Acts 4:4), the Ethiopian eunuch (Acts 8), Lydia (Acts 16), and the Philippian jailor (Acts 16). However, this is an argument from silence. No verse says they did not receive the Spirit. The Bible simply does not go into detail to describe all these conversions. Just as the Gospels record only representative miracles and events in Christ's ministry for lack of space (John 21:25), so Acts describes only a sampling of the important conversion experiences. God inspired Luke to choose five accounts of the Spirit baptism that would have great symbolic significance for later ages. Luke recorded enough to establish a precedent for every situation so that it was not necessary to record every other case or to describe other conversions in detail.*

Even so, there is still evidence that all converts received the Spirit. The 5000 'believed' and Lydia 'believed', and true belief leads to receiving the Spirit. The eunuch and the jailer both received an experience that caused rejoicing, which probably was the result of the baptism of the Spirit. [18]

We know the gospel is the death, burial, and resurrection of Jesus Christ, and still many times throughout Paul's epistles he just mentions the gospel without explaining what it is. Why? Because his readers understand what the gospel is *(1 Corinthians 15:1-4).*

Final Thoughts

Receiving the Gift of the Holy Ghost is a real true biblical experience that was not just for the 1st Century Church. You may say, "This hasn't happened to me; I haven't received it; I haven't spoken in tongues." The simple answer is if you desire the gift of God's Spirit living inside of you, then it is yours for the asking!

He is the Holy Spirit, who leads into all truth. The world cannot receive him, because it isn't looking for him and doesn't recognize him. But you know him, because he lives with you now and later will be in you. (John 14:17 NLT)

I hope that this chapter has enlightened the scripture and brought out that there is more to the salvation message than just believing. God is showing us that there is more. My intention is not to take anything away from someone's experience, but to encourage you to search the scriptures and add to your experience. God sometimes brings us along in stages in our walk with Him until we are ready to receive all that He has for us.

As a young Catholic boy, I had always believed that Jesus Christ was the Son of God and that He had died for our sins. I was told that I received the Holy Ghost during the Sacrament of Confirmation, although there was no biblical experience connected to it. But when I heard that I could receive this same gift today that the apostles did 2000years ago, I wanted it. And when I repented of my sins and prayed at an old fashion altar, God filled me with the Holy Ghost, and I spoke in tongues. Receiving the Holy Spirit was the greatest experience of my life! I felt that God inspired me to write this book so that others would hear the things that are written and would desire to receive it too. Everyone should desire to receive this wonderful gift of God.

10

CHAPTER 29

The Book of Acts ends abruptly. Paul arrived at Rome and called the local Jewish leaders and told them the story of how he was arrested in Jerusalem though he did nothing wrong. The Romans tried and released him finding no cause worthy of a death sentence. However, the Jewish leaders protested that decision and so Paul felt the necessity to appeal to Caesar. After he arrived in Rome, Paul told the Jews in Rome that he had arrived and was ready to explain to them what he believed: that the hope of Israel, the Messiah, had already come.

The scripture records the words of the Jewish brethren who came to hear what Paul had to say:

> *And they said unto him, We neither received letters out of Judaea concerning thee, neither any of the brethren that came shewed or spake any harm of thee. But we desire to hear of thee what thou thinkest: for as concerning this sect, we know that every where it is spoken against. And when they had appointed him a day, there came many to him into his lodging; to whom he expounded and testified the kingdom of God, persuading them concerning Jesus, both out of the law of Moses, and out of the*

prophets, from morning till evening. And some believed the things which were spoken, and some believed not. And when they agreed not among themselves, they departed... (Acts 28:21-25)

Paul then berated his Jewish brethren:

...after that Paul had spoken one word, Well spake the Holy Ghost by Esaias the prophet unto our fathers, Saying, Go unto this people, and say, Hearing ye shall hear, and shall not understand; and seeing ye shall see, and not perceive: For the heart of this people is waxed gross, and their ears are dull of hearing, and their eyes have they closed; lest they should see with their eyes, and hear with their ears, and understand with their heart, and should be converted, and I should heal them. Be it known therefore unto you, that the salvation of God is sent unto the Gentiles, and that they will hear it. (Acts 28:25-28)

So, the Book of Acts ends with these words:

And Paul dwelt two whole years in his own hired house, and received all that came in unto him, Preaching the kingdom of God, and teaching those things which concern the Lord Jesus Christ, with all confidence, no man forbidding him. (Acts 28:30-31)

I know, this seems like a strange name for a chapter, *Chapter 29*. So why did I name it so? The reason is because the Book of the Acts of the Apostles does not end. I'm writing this chapter about the continuation of the Church of the 1st Century. No, I am not declaring that my writing is by divine inspiration. I am not adding to the Word of God. I am simply saying that we are the 21st Century Apostolic Church and we preach the same Gospel that Peter, Paul, Philip and all the other Apostolic Christians preached. We have the same Holy Spirit along with all the power of the 1st Century Church. We still believe that God is healing people today and performing miracles. We believe that we are living in the last days before the second coming of the

Lord Jesus Christ and because of this we should live our lives according to the teachings of the Bible and not follow the philosophies of this world.

And how are we supposed to be living in this *29th Chapter of Acts*? I believe that the Epistles give us the answer to this question. We are certainly to live differently than people in the world do. After all, what would attract the world to the Church if we were just like them? Why would they want to become like us if we live according to the way they do? We should attract them because we are different. This would also cause some to hate us. When we live according to the scripture, we will be treated like Jesus was treated. He was loved by those who believed in Him and hated by the world.

In Romans Chapter 12, Paul lays out some good principles for Christians to live by. These are things that are found in many other passages of scripture, so they give us a good foundation for living in the *29th Chapter of Acts*. Our first responsibility is to love and serve our God.

And so, dear brothers and sisters, I plead with you to give your bodies to God because of all he has done for you. Let them be a living and holy sacrifice—the kind he will find acceptable. This is truly the way to worship him. (Romans 12:1 NLT)

Loving God First

Paul is pleading, appealing to us through the scripture to give ourselves completely to God in our worship of Him. Our lives should be a living and holy sacrifice, totally dedicated and committed to Him, something that God would find acceptable. God has done so much for us and we should be loyal to Him and obedient to His Word. We should love God with our whole heart.

Someone once asked Jesus what was the greatest commandment in the law? His answer was: "Thou shalt love the Lord thy God with all thy heart, and with all thy soul, and with all thy mind" (Matthew

22:37). This is the 1ˢᵗ commandment in the law. We find it in Deuteronomy 6:4-5:

> *Hear, O Israel: The LORD our God is one LORD:* ⁵ *And thou shalt love the LORD thy God with all thine heart, and with all thy soul, and with all thy might. (Deuteronomy 6:4-5)*

To love someone with all of your heart, soul, mind, and might is to love with every fiber of your being. In this verse, Jesus uses the Greek word "agapao" (agape) which is the highest form of love. This is a self-sacrificing love like the love Jesus has for us. It is this love that caused God to become a man so that He could die on the cross for us. We should have died, but Jesus took our place: He became our Substitutionary Sacrifice.

But what does this mean for us? This means we must love God supremely and there is no other person, place or thing that we adore more than God. Not mother or father, not our spouse or our children, not any other person no matter how close the relationship. God wants our First Love! This also involves submitting to God's will and purpose before our own. This is a love that comes directly from our hearts and it means that we love Him with all the faculties and inner might that we have. It means that we prefer nothing before Him.

Loving Our Neighbor

> *A second is equally important: 'Love your neighbor as yourself.' The entire law and all the demands of the prophets are based on these two commandments. (Matthew 22:39-40 NLT)*

This is the second commandment in the law, but it is also another commandment that Jesus gave us to follow. He said that this second commandment was equally important as the first. We are commanded by Jesus to love one another. This deals with our horizontal relationships. We cannot have a proper relationship with God if we don't have love for all people. The Ten Commandments and all the other Old Testament laws are summarized by these two commandments: to love God and to love our neighbor. If we will fulfill these two commandments, we would keep all of the others also *(Matthew 22:37-40)*.

Love is the greatest commandment of all. 1 Corinthians 13 is known as the "love" chapter because it tells us that without love everything else is useless, powerless, and has no lasting purpose. Without love our greatest efforts fail. I could have a great and powerful ministry, even a prophetic one, but if I don't have love, I am nothing. All of our good deeds will profit us nothing if we don't have love. Faith, hope, and charity (love) are three of the greatest virtues, but the greatest of all is Love. Following the 13th Chapter of 1st Corinthians is how we should strive to live among our neighbors in this *29th Chapter of Acts*:

> *Love is patient and kind. Love is not jealous or boastful or proud or rude. It does not demand its own way. It is not irritable, and it keeps no record of being wronged. It does not rejoice about injustice but rejoices whenever the truth wins out. Love never gives up, never loses faith, is always hopeful, and endures through every circumstance. (1 Corinthians 13:4-7 NLT).*

We all should make a firm commitment to live the way Jesus said we should live. In Matthew 7:12, He gave what many of us today call the *Golden Rule:* "Do to others whatever you would like them to do to you. This is the essence of all that is taught in the law and the prophets" *(Matthew 7:12 NLT)*.

What a great place this world would be if we all tried to treat one another like we want to be treated. Who likes to be mistreated? Who likes to be the victim of a crime? Who likes to be verbally abused? Most people would answer "not me" to most of those questions. But that's exactly the point. If you wouldn't like to be treated in a certain way, then don't treat someone else that way.

Take a moment and think about this. If we would do according to Jesus' teaching on the Golden Rule, then there would be no more war, murders, thefts, lying. There would be no more racism, social injustice, abuse, slavery or mistreatment of any kind. Now that is the kind of planet I would like to live on. Unfortunately, that is not planet Earth!

The Word of God

Two things that are vital for living out this new life that God has birthed in us are the Word of God and Prayer. Jesus told us about the Word of God and how necessary it is for us. He used the Word Himself while being tempted of the devil. He said that man doesn't live by bread alone but by every word that comes from the mouth of God *(Matthew 4:11)*. He once said: "Heaven and earth shall pass away, but my words shall not pass away" *(Matthew 24:35)*.

Toward the end of the Sermon on the Mount, Jesus gives us a parable about two persons and their response to His Words. He likened the one who was obedient to a person who built his house on a rock *(His Words)*. The other was building on sand. He said when the storm came the house built on the rock stood, while the other collapsed with a great crash *(Matthew 7:24-27)*. In 2 Timothy 3, the Apostle Paul wrote:

> *And that from a child thou hast known the holy scriptures, which are able to make thee wise unto salvation through faith which is in Christ Jesus. All scripture is given by inspiration of God, and is profitable for doctrine, for reproof, for correction, for instruction in righteousness: That the man of God may be perfect, thoroughly furnished unto all good works. (2 Timothy 3:15-17)*

God's Word is inspired. Every word of scripture is "God-breathed," that is, it is a part of the creative breath of God. It came directly from God. God breathed out the Word much like He did when He created the world *(Psalm 33:6)*.

> *Knowing this first, that no prophecy of the scripture is of any private interpretation. For the prophecy came not in old time by the will of man: but*

holy men of God spake as they were moved by the Holy Ghost. (2 Peter 1:20-21)

God inspired holy men to bring us the scriptures. Peter tells us that God's Word was not an invention of man. This was not man's commentary nor did it originate from man. The Holy Spirit moved upon men, greatly influencing them to write. They were not writing their own thoughts but their minds were illuminated by God so that He gave them the knowledge of things they could never have known, divine things. That is why the Word is infallible. That is why the Word is without error. That is why it is the Truth!

God has given us His Word so that we may profit by it in this New Testament era. The Word is our major source of teaching, which is doctrine. The Word reproves, corrects and instructs us. The scripture is used to equip and prepare the Christian for every good work in God's Kingdom (*2 Timothy 3:17*). Paul also wrote:

Let the message about Christ, in all its richness, fill your lives. Teach and counsel each other with all the wisdom he gives. Sing psalms and hymns and spiritual songs to God with thankful hearts. And whatever you do or say, do it as a representative of the Lord Jesus, giving thanks through him to God the Father." (Colossians 3:16-17 NLT)

We see the admonition from the Apostle Paul that the Word spoken by Jesus should be hidden away in the heart and mind of the Christian and that it should be used to teach and train one another in all spiritual things. We should lay aside or "fling off" all the elements of our past sinful lives and as new born Christians we should crave or thirst for the spiritual milk of the Word of God so that we may grow to a full and complete salvation (*1 Peter 2:1-2*).

Prayer

Prayer is communing with God and is the most important thing a believer can learn to do. Without prayer we have no communication with God. Prayer is our lifeline to God and it is how we establish a relationship with Him. In prayer we praise and worship the God who created us for who He is and for what He has done. It is in prayer that we ask God for the things we need and it is where we also petition Our Lord to come to the aid of our brothers and sisters in Christ. As children of God living in the *29th Chapter of Acts*, we should pray daily and often because prayer is powerful! Prayer moves God! It is in prayer that we receive power from God to resist sin and defeat the devil. Denzil Holman wrote this about prayer:

> *Prayer is powerful, because it invokes God, who is omnipotent, or unlimited in power. When we pray, we look past our limitations, helplessness, and circumstances and look unto Jesus, who has all power and has vast resources.* [1]

Jesus was the greatest example that taught us of our need to pray. Though He was God manifested in flesh, Jesus spent complete nights in prayer after a full day of healing people of their sicknesses and diseases. Limited by His humanity, Jesus needed that continual renewal of the Spirit. "And it came to pass in those days, that he went out into a mountain to pray, and continued all night in prayer to God" *(Luke 6:12)*.

Throughout the Gospels Jesus teaches us:

- How to pray *(Matthew 6:7,9-13)*.
- When to pray *(Luke 22:40)*.
- Where to pray *(Matthew 6:6)*.
- What to pray for *(Mark 11:24)*.
- Who to pray for *(Matthew 5:44)*.
- He even gives us some prayer points *(Matthew 9:38, 26:41; Mark 13:33; Luke 10:2, 21:36)*.

Prayer was a central and supreme part of the first Century Christians lifestyle: "And they continued stedfastly in the apostles' doctrine and fellowship, and in breaking of bread, and in prayers *(Acts 2:42)*. Prayer was a continual practice of the Apostles and New Testament saints *(Acts 10:9, Romans 8:26, 1 Corinthians 14:15, 1 Thessalonians 5:17,25, 1 Timothy 2:8, James 5:15-16)*.

E.M. Bounds was a great man of prayer, and he has written a classic collection on the Christian's privilege of prayer. In the first chapter of his book, he writes:

> *The most important lesson we can learn is how to pray. Indeed, we must pray so that our prayers take hold of God. The man who has done the most and the best praying is the most immortal, because prayers do not die... Prayer is God' settled and singular condition to move ahead His Son's Kingdom. Therefore, the believer who is the most highly skilled in prayer will do the most for God. Men are to pray---- to pray for the advance of God's cause. The one who can wield the power of prayer is the strong one, the holy one, in Christ's Kingdom.* [2]

Nothing can keep you closer to God than a consistent prayer life. These are just a few examples of how important prayer was to the 1st Century Church. We should ask ourselves, "Do we look at prayer the same way?" If not, why not?

Faith

What is faith? The Bible describes it this way: "Now faith is the substance of things hoped for, the evidence of things not seen" *(Hebrews 11:1)*. The Amplified Bible defines faith as an assurance or a confirmation of things that we are hoping for. It is the proof of things we don't see and it is the conviction of their reality. Faith is perceiving as real fact what is not revealed to the senses. John MacArthur explains it like this in his commentary: "Faith is living in a hope that is so real it gives absolute assurance." [3]

We are demonstrating true faith when we believe that God is going to fulfill His promises to us without seeing even a shred of evidence. And this is the kind of faith that can move mountains. Faith is so important because as Hebrews 6 says:

> But without faith it is impossible to please him: for he that cometh to God must believe that he is, and that he is a rewarder of them that diligently seek him. (Hebrews 11:6)

Faith is believing what God says is true! Acting like God is telling the truth! Having faith is vital for every Christian.

- We are saved through faith (*Ephesians 2:8*).
- Miracles happen when faith is released (*Acts 3:16*).
- The just live by faith (*Romans 1:17*).
- We are justified by faith (*Romans 3:28*).
- Our faith is counted for righteousness (*Romans 4:5*).
- Faith gives us access into God's grace (*Romans 5:2*).
- We receive the promise of the Spirit through faith (*Galatians 3:14*).
- The shield of faith quenches all the fiery darts of the wicked (*Ephesians 6:16*).
- The joy of faith (*Philippians 1:25*).
- We rise with Jesus through the faith of the operation of God. (*Colossians 2:12*).
- We put on the breastplate of faith and love (*1 Thessalonians 5:8*).
- We are nourished up in the words of faith and of good doctrine (*1 Timothy 4:6*).
- We fight the fight of faith (*1 Timothy 6:12*).
- We have salvation through faith which is in Christ Jesus (*2 Timothy 3:15*).
- Faith without works is dead (*James 2:20*).

Don't Conform to This World

And be not conformed to this world: but be ye transformed by the renewing of your mind, that ye may prove what is that good, and acceptable, and perfect, will of God. (Romans 12:2)

Paul is cautioning us not to live like the heathen world does. We should not imitate the behavior and customs of our world. David Bernard says in his commentary on Romans:

Not only does this involve worldly activities and dress, it also involves worldly value systems, standards of success, modes of operation, and lifestyles. Worldliness is the lust of the flesh, the lust of the eyes, and the pride of life. (1 John 2:15) [4]

So, we stop allowing ourselves to be molded by our present society. As Daniel Seagraves writes in *Living by Faith:* "It is…a command to stop allowing one's self to be shaped and molded by contemporary godless society [5]". Instead, we need to allow God to transform our lives through the renewing of our minds by His Word. This will give us new insights into truth and new attitudes for us to live by. We must get rid of some of the baggage we brought into this new life in Christ.

Throw off your old sinful nature and your former way of life, which is corrupted by lust and deception. Instead, let the Spirit renew your thoughts and attitudes. Put on your new nature, created to be like God—truly righteous and holy. (Ephesians 4:22-24 NLT)

Paul sounds a similar warning to the Romans when he wrote: "So remove your dark deeds like dirty clothes, and put on the shining armor of right living" *(Romans13:12-13 NLT)*. Paul is telling us to strip ourselves of or put off our former sinful life with all its corruption and lust. Stop participating in wild parties, sexual promiscuity, deviant lifestyles. Stop your immoral living and drunkenness. Turn away from various forms of sinful living. We should be renewed in the spirit of our minds having renewed thoughts and attitudes. And we should put on that new nature created in righteousness and holiness. We should no longer covet or be jealous and envious of those who possess more than we do. We should stop arguing and fighting among ourselves and love one another as Jesus loved us. We should tell the truth and stop telling lies or bearing false witness because all liars will have their part in the lake of fire (*Revelation 21:8*).

We should love one another sincerely and be humble and honest in all we do, especially in the evaluation of ourselves. We should live in harmony with one another and never look down upon someone else thinking that we are better than him. We must work hard and serve God enthusiastically. We should remember that we are all a part of one body and we unite together for the good of that body (*our head is Christ*). We all pool our talents together and by doing so the body functions as one.

Unity

> Unity in the Kingdom of God among the brethren is a good and a pleasant thing according to the scripture: *"Behold, how good and how pleasant it is for brethren to dwell together in unity!" (Psalm 133:1)*.

Jesus taught His disciples to be united as one. He prayed that they would all be one (*John 17:11*) like He and His Father are one. Paul wrote in 2 Corinthians 13:11 "That they should be of one mind and live in peace and in 1 Corinthians 1:10 he wrote:

> *Now I beseech you, brethren, by the name of our Lord Jesus Christ, that ye all speak the same thing, and that there be no divisions among you; but that ye be perfectly joined together in the same mind and in the same judgment. (1 Corinthians 1: 10)*

Oh, if we could only realize the peace we could have on the earth today if we would have unity in the Body of Christ. On the contrary, when there is division in the body it is destructive and it causes disunity. Division was fully entrenched in the Church of Corinth. Paul knew this and he tried to help the Corinthians to understand that unless they solved this problem of division within the body, the church would never function as it should. Jesus once spoke of a feuding house when He was accused of performing miracles by the power of Satan. He said:

> ...Every kingdom divided against itself is brought to desolation; and every city or house divided against itself shall not stand... (Matthew 12:25)

> ...Any kingdom that is divided against itself is being brought to desolation and laid waste, and no city or house divided against itself will last or continue to stand. (Matthew 12:25 AMP)

That is why Satan loves to destroy a church that is unified. He is a destroyer, and division is his weapon of destruction. He will cause dissention and division and he will try to drive wedges between the members of the body by using various things such as politics or jealousy. He likes to spread disagreement among the people and cause some to be offended by other members of the congregation thereby causing splits within the Body of Christ.

In the Book of Acts, the Bible speaks to us as being in "one accord." Before the Holy Ghost was poured out on the Day of Pentecost the scripture states that the one hundred and twenty in the upper room were in "one accord" and in supplication (*Acts 1:14*). While waiting for the Promise of the Father they were in "one accord" (*Acts 2:1*). In Acts 2:46 they were continuing daily in "one accord" worshipping in the Temple. They again were found worshipping the Lord in Acts 4:24 in "one accord." Many signs and wonders were done by the Apostles as the people were in "one accord." In Samaria the people in "one accord" gave heed to the things Philip spoke and the miracles he did (*Acts 8:6*). In Acts 15 the men came together in "one accord" to deal with a situation that had developed in the church. And finally, Paul wrote to the Philippians and said: "Fulfil ye my joy, that ye be likeminded, having the same love, being of one accord, of one mind" *(Philippians 2:2).*

And to the Ephesian Church he wrote: "Endeavouring to keep the unity of the Spirit in the bond of peace" *(Ephesians 4:3).* What does this mean? Simply: United we stand and divided we fall! And we should strive to keep the *unity* of the body until Jesus comes again!

Living Holy Lives

God is holy. He alone is completely holy! Holiness is a basic characteristic of God. This means He is absolutely pure and perfectly moral. He is completely different from anything or anyone else in the world.

> *But as he which hath called you is holy, so be ye holy in all manner of conversation; Because it is written, Be ye holy; for I am holy. (1 Peter 1:15-16)*

God is not only holy, but He wants us to live holy lives also. But we are not morally perfect beings due to our sin nature and our sinful actions and deeds. And we certainly are not absolutely pure. So, what does holiness mean for us? How can we obey the scripture by being "holy in all manner of conversation," which is dealing with our behavior? In his book, *Practical Holiness, A Second Look,* David Bernard states:

> *Specifically, holiness consists of two components: (1) separation from sin and worldliness and (2) dedication to God and His will...Holiness means we cannot love this ungodly world system, identify with it, become attached to the things in it, or participate in its sinful pleasures and activities.* [6]

The Bible also contains verses regarding this thought:

> *Follow peace with all men, and holiness, without which no man shall see the Lord... (Hebrews 12:14)*

> *That ye put off concerning the former conversation the old man, which is corrupt according to the deceitful lusts; And be renewed in the spirit of your mind; And that ye put on the new man, which after God is created in righteousness and true holiness. (Ephesians 4:22-24)*

Holiness begins on the inside when someone is filled with the Holy Ghost. Then as we continue to walk with God and obey His will, God's holy presence will begin to affect our outward man. Then we will desire to put away the things of this world, even laying down some "weights," things that are not necessarily sinful but that keep us too attached to this world. We must work at living a holy life if we want to see the Lord. Paul is saying that we must "put off" the past behavior that existed before we were filled with the Holy Ghost. We must forsake the old life of sin while at the same time letting God's Spirit renew our thoughts and attitudes. Then we must "put on" the new nature that is righteous and holy. Brian Kinsey writes: "Putting on the new man means taking on the nature of Jesus Christ Himself. The new birth imparts a nature that is born in the image of Jesus Christ [7]." He continues by saying that after we have become brand new by the new birth, we must:

> *Adopt a new way of life with a new set of principles. As our new nature gains greater control over our actions, we are gradually transformed to take on the character of Jesus Christ.* [8]

And what does the Bible say about this new way of life?

> *But clothe yourself with the Lord Jesus Christ (the Messiah), and make no provision for [indulging] the flesh [put a stop to thinking about the evil cravings of your physical nature] to [gratify its] desires (lusts). (Romans 13:13 AMP)*

Instead, clothe yourself with the presence of the Lord Jesus Christ. And don't let yourself think about ways to indulge your evil desires. (Romans 13:14 NLT)

We Must Preach the Gospel

The Gospel of Jesus Christ is defined for us by the Apostle Paul in 1 Corinthians 15:1-4:

Moreover, brethren, I declare unto you the gospel which I preached unto you, which also ye have received, and wherein ye stand; By which also ye are saved, if ye keep in memory what I preached unto you, unless ye have believed in vain. For I delivered unto you first of all that which I also received, how that Christ died for our sins according to the scriptures And that he was buried, and that he rose again the third day according to the scriptures... (1 Corinthians 15:1-4)

This was the gospel that Peter preached to the Jews. This was the gospel that Paul preached to the Gentiles. And this is the same gospel we preach today. God's Word does not change and neither has this gospel which has been preached throughout the world for about 2,000 years. God's power is released when the true gospel is preached. That is the way it was in the first century in Acts 1, and God's power is still being released to save and to heal in this 21st Century in the *29th Chapter of Acts.*

Through mighty signs and wonders, by the power of the Spirit of God; so that from Jerusalem, and round about unto Illyricum, I have fully preached the gospel of Christ. (Romans 15:19)

For I am not ashamed of the gospel of Christ: for it is the power of God unto salvation to every one that believeth; to the Jew first, and also to the Greek. (Romans 1:16)

> *For our gospel came not unto you in word only, but also in power, and in the Holy Ghost, and in much assurance; as ye know what manner of men we were among you for your sake. (1 Thessalonians 1:5)*

Even today when the gospel is preached, people are being born again of water and Spirit, receiving the baptism of the Holy Ghost speaking in unknown tongues as the Spirit of God gives the utterance. People are being healed of sicknesses and diseases just like it happened in the 1st Century. I have recorded some of those miracles in Chapter Three of this book. And there have been many more that could have been written.

Why Must We Preach the Gospel?

The Apostle Paul, who was probably the greatest evangelist that ever lived, spent his life, after his conversion, preaching the gospel in order to save those that were lost. He had such an insatiable burden for the souls of men that it led him to go on three great missionary journeys in which he jeopardized his life for the gospel. He was the first of all those who spend their lives on mission field today. He did so because he knew that the gospel had to be preached to men and women who were held captive by the devil due to their unbelief. He preached to open the eyes of those who were blind to the truth of God's salvation.

> *But if our gospel be hid, it is hid to them that are lost: In whom the god of this world hath blinded the minds of them which believe not, lest the light of the glorious gospel of Christ, who is the image of God, should shine unto them. For we preach not ourselves, but Christ Jesus the Lord; and ourselves your servants for Jesus' sake. For God, who commanded the light to shine out of darkness, hath shined in our hearts, to give the light of the knowledge of the glory of God in the face of Jesus Christ. (2 Corinthians 4:3-6)*

This is the reason that we must preach the gospel today. Our day is not much different from the day of the Apostle Paul. Men are still bound by sin. Evil men and women still live among us. Satan is still blinding the eyes of people keeping them in unbelief. People die and many have never heard the gospel preached unto them. Young teenagers and old people, rich and poor, minorities and the majorities, are taking their own lives because they are without any hope in this evil world. Drug and alcohol addiction claims thousands of lives every year. We live in a desperate world, a world that needs to hear the gospel preached in its entirety and simplicity. This is why Paul had such a burden to preach the gospel.

> *For though I preach the gospel, I have nothing to glory of: for necessity is laid upon me; yea, woe is unto me, if I preach not the gospel! (1 Corinthians 9:16)*

Paul was called by God to be a minister of the gospel. God said he chose him to be a special messenger to bear His name (*Jesus*) before the Gentiles and because of this Paul would suffer many things (*Acts 9:15-16*). This was not a calling that Paul took lightly. He literally gave his life to fulfill his calling. He said: "Yea, so have I strived to preach the gospel, not where Christ was named, lest I should build upon another man's foundation..." *(Romans 15:20)*.

- He wasn't interested in making a name for himself or building an empire in his own name.
- He didn't want to start a work where another minister started (*Romans 15:20*). He was a pioneer of his day. We would call him a church planter today.
- He was compelled to preach the gospel because he had been given a commission by the Lord Jesus when he was converted (*Acts 9:15-16*).
- He said he had a great sense of obligation to people in both the civilized world and the rest of the world, to those who were educated and uneducated. "...I am made all things to

all men, that I might by all means save some" *(1 Corinthians 9:22-23).*
- He understood that God's power was at work in the gospel to make people right in His sight *(Romans 1:14-17).*

These are examples of what a humble man the Apostle Paul was. As John MacArthur explains:

The primary purpose of Paul's not taking full advantage of his Christian liberty was that [he] might win the more. He deeply believed that "he who is wise wins souls" (Prov. 11: 30) and was willing to do anything and to sacrifice anything to win people to Jesus Christ. As far as his rights were concerned he was free from all men, but because of his love for all men he would gladly limit those rights for their sakes. He had, figuratively, become a slave to all... he would not change the least truth in the least way in order to satisfy anyone. But he would condescend in any way for anyone if that would in any way help bring him to Christ. He would never set aside a truth of the gospel, but he would gladly restrict his liberty in the gospel. He would not offend Jew, Gentile, or those weak in understanding. [9]

All of Paul's laboring and struggling was for one great purpose: to see souls saved and to see them become disciples of Christ (*Colossians 1:28*). And this is exactly how we should be ministering today. The Life Application Bible Commentary states:

Paul was willing to go to great lengths to meet people where they were. He had one focus: I do all this for the sake of the gospel, that I may share in its blessings. Paul's life focused on taking the gospel to an unbelieving world. He did not preach with pride, counting the number of converts; Instead, he preached with love for the gospel and for people, so that in the end, he and all believers could share together in the blessings of knowing Christ. [10]

Our chief concern should be to reach every person we can reach and not only bring them to the waters of baptism in Jesus' Name but to help them to mature in Jesus Christ. The born-again experience is only the beginning. Once someone is converted, the discipleship portion of one's life begins and that is where the working and struggling sometimes also begins. I wonder what the Apostle Paul would think about the Church in America today? What would he think about the Church in the world today? We can only wonder what kind of letter he would have written to us.

Final Thoughts

There are so many other things that could have been included in this chapter. The Bible is an unending source of knowledge, encouragement, and instruction in Christian Living that you can find something new to write about every time you read it. These are just a few more thoughts from the epistles of the Apostle Paul.

- Rejoice in hope and be patient in times of trouble, suffering, and tribulation (*Romans 12:12*).
- Pray without ceasing (1 *Thessalonians 5:17*).
- Always be willing to help those in need (*Galatians 6:10*).
- Rejoice with those who rejoice and weep with them that weep (*Philippians 2:16, 4:4*).
- Live in harmony and humility with one another – don't be a snob! Be humble and don't be a know it all (*2 Corinthians 2:17, Philippians 2:3-4, Romans 13:13; Philippians 4:8*).
- Don't repay evil for evil and do what is honorable. Try to live in peace with all men (*Romans 12:17-18*).
- Don't seek revenge when wronged but let God be your avenger (*Romans 12:19*).
- Don't be overcome by evil but conquer it by doing good (*Romans 12:20*).

I don't know exactly what it was like to live as a Christian in the 1st Century. I imagine that it must have been much like life is today, except of course without all the technology we have at our disposal. I know that there was much persecution in the early days of Christianity where Christians lost their lives for Jesus Christ, as there is today in certain parts of the world. I know from the Word of God that Christians had to deal with false doctrines and false teachers. I know from the scripture that Satan was very much involved in leading men astray by offering them an alternate way of life, and keeping men and women blinded in darkness due to their unbelief.

However, like the Apostle Paul, we have the words of life that can set people free. We have God's Word of truth that can open the mind and hearts of people to believe that God can save their soul. We have a Gospel that has the power to redeem all mankind from their sin. We may not all be the Apostle Paul, or Peter, or John, or Philip, but we all have a ministry that God has entrusted to us. Like Paul we must be compelled to fulfill the ministry that God has given to us. The only hope of our dying and sin sick world is for you and me to share Jesus Christ and bring His saving message to our world, helping others to enter the great Kingdom of God!

11
THE END OF THE AGE

We are standing on the precipice of the Second Coming of the Lord Jesus Christ. Why do I say this? One reason is because the Bible indicates that we are very near the Second Coming of Our Lord, as I will endeavor to show in this chapter. The other reason is when I look at current events, they are telling me that Bible prophecy is being fulfilled right before our eyes and that we are very near the end of this age.

The Tower of Babel

In Genesis Chapter 11 we read about the Tower of Babel:

And they said, Come, let us build us a city and a tower whose top reaches into the sky, and let us make a name for ourselves, lest we be scattered over the whole earth. (Genesis 11:4 AMP)

This agreement among the people of the land was in direct rebellion against God's word to Noah as they all exited the Ark. God told

Noah to: "Now be fruitful and multiply and repopulate the earth" *(Genesis 9:7 NLT)*.

After the flood, God gave man the right to eat animal flesh and scripture says that the fear of man would be upon all animals *(Genesis 9:2)* because now man would hunt animals for food.

One of the most notable individuals after the flood was Nimrod. His name means, "he rebelled." He was the grandson of Noah's son Ham, and he was named a "mighty hunter before the Lord" *(Genesis 10:9)*. Henry Morris writes this about Nimrod:

> *Nimrod became a 'mighty tyrant in the face of Jehovah'. He was a 'hunter' in the sense that he was implacable [ruthless] in searching out and persuading men to obey his will.* [1]

Although the wild animals were not considered to be a real source of danger to the human population, anyone who would be able to protect the population from them would acclaim hero status. Henry Morris continues to say:

> *That there was probably no genuine danger to mankind from the animals, however, is evident from God's promise to put the 'fear and dread' of man on all of them (Genesis 9:2), so that the deliberate hunting and slaughter of them was 'against the Lord' (verse 9, literally). It was by this means, however, that Nimrod apparently acquired his great reputation and rose to a position as a world leader of the time.* [2]

Besides being a successful hunter, Nimrod was also a builder of cities. He created walled cities for the people for protection. Then he organized the cities into kingdoms. There was only one problem: Nimrod was an ungodly ruler. David S. Norris writes of Nimrod in this fashion:

> *That man was Nimrod, and his kingdom was Babel. The Bible makes this cryptic statement: Nimrod was a 'hunter before the Lord.' Now, there is a*

whole lot more to such a statement that might be understood at first glance. Tradition tells us there is so much more. Certainly, Nimrod had prowess before the Lord, yet Nimrod's prowess was 'in sin.' Talmudic interpretations describe Nimrod as one who 'led all the world in rebellion against him. [God.].' Christian interpretations likewise report the same. [3]

This kingdom of Nimrod (Babel) is the first mentioned kingdom in the Bible, and it was here, in Babel, that mankind came together to rebel against God. The Tower of Babel was the first Satanically inspired, manmade collective action of outright rebellion against God.

Satan is the great deceiver. That is what he does. He has deceived mankind from the beginning, drawing people away from worshipping God to worshiping himself. The Book of Revelation says he is one "which deceiveth the whole world" *(Revelation 12:9)*. It was here in Babel, under the leadership of Nimrod, that men built a tower to reach unto the heavens.

...and it came to pass, as they Journeyed from the east, that they found a plain in the land of Shinar; and they dwelt there... And they said, Go to, let us build us a city and a tower, whose top may reach unto heaven; and let us make us a name, lest we be scattered abroad upon the face of the whole earth. (Genesis. 11:2,4)

Babel became the center of the world's false religions. This is where it all began and it was here that the City of Babylon was built. James M. Boice writes in his book, *Genesis Volume 1, An Expositional Commentary*:

The religion of the tower was actually a satanic attempt to direct the worship of the human race to himself and those former angels who, having rebelled against God, were now already demons. [4]

When God confounded their languages while they were building the tower (*Genesis11:6-8*), this false religion spread throughout the world. Mystery Babylon in the Book of Revelation had its start at the Tower of Babel *(Revelation 17:5)*.

It is also believed that Nimrod is the first type of an Antichrist, and his rebellion against God was also the first attempt at a One World Governing System. In the last days, and very likely in our day, we will witness the rise of a One World Government, One World Religion and a One World Economy that will be led by the Antichrist of the Book of Revelation, but it all had its beginning at the Tower of Babel. Henry Morris writes:

> *Furthermore, the development of this system of idolatry and Satan worship was accompanied by an attempt to unify all mankind under one government...Nimrod not only set up a military dictatorship but also established a priestly oligarchy, in which he himself was chief priest and later the chief object of worship.* [5]

What's Going on in Our World?

This One World Government System seems to be coming to pass very quickly today. Our world is in turmoil. Mankind is growing more and more wicked. Just like the Bible tells us, these times will be perilous times *(very difficult and hard to bear)* because of man's sinfulness:

> *BUT UNDERSTAND this, that in the last days will come (set in) perilous times of great stress and trouble [hard to deal with and hard to bear]. For people will be lovers of self and [utterly] self-centered, lovers of money and aroused by an inordinate [greedy] desire for wealth, proud and arrogant and contemptuous boasters. They will be abusive (blasphemous, scoffing), disobedient to parents, ungrateful, unholy and profane. [They will be] without natural [human] affection (callous and inhuman), relentless (admitting of no truce or appeasement); [they will be] slanderers (false accusers, troublemakers), intemperate and loose in morals and conduct, uncontrolled and fierce, haters of good. [They will be] treacherous [betray-*

ers], rash, [and] inflated with self-conceit. [They will be] lovers of sensual pleasures and vain amusements more than and rather than lovers of God. For [although] they hold a form of piety (true religion), they deny and reject and are strangers to the power of it [their conduct belies the genuineness of their profession]. Avoid [all] such people [turn away from them]. (2 Timothy 3:1-5 AMP)

Writing his second pastoral epistle to Timothy, Paul warns him that the last days will be perilous, because of the spiritual condition of men's hearts and the attitudes of ungodly people. People would be very difficult to deal with causing great stress and trouble. If this prevailing spirit was present during the first century, we should not be surprised at the moral degeneration of our society today.

How true this is of our day. Love of self and self-centeredness is widespread today. Greed, love of money, is ruling in our society. Children are abusive and disobedient to parents and elders and they are ungrateful and think that the world owes them everything. Lying and bearing false witness is a daily occurrence within our news media today. You have to really work hard to find truth in journalism. We are a society that is hooked on sensual pleasures and amusements. Pornography is a billion-dollar business addicting both men, women, and young teens. Even among ministers of all denominations, pornography is widespread. Today, more than any other time, anything goes. Even among the religious there is deception. 2 Timothy 3:5 says that they have, "a form of godliness but they deny the power thereof."

War and unrest are expanding upon the whole world. War between Russia and the Ukraine is in the news every day since the conflict had escalated in February, 2022. In fact, just today (Dec.16,2022) I have read this, *"In a recent meeting Putin said, 'In terms of the threat of nuclear war, you are right: Such threat is increasing'"* [6]. That same website also reported that the "NATO Secretary-General said that there was a 'real possibility' of a full-fledged war between NATO and Russia if things go wrong."

The Middle East is a powder keg. Israel is in a constant battle with the raiding Palestinians, and Syrians. And of course, there is always a threat of war between Israel and Iran. There is even unrest in the West with China wanting to reannex Taiwan but the Taiwanese want no part of it. China has threatened that they will go to war over Taiwan and will fight against anyone who will stand against them. Besides the U.S., there are also other nations who are not willing to see this happen. This could involve nations such as Japan, India, Korea and even Australia.

Jesus said that the days before His coming would be like the days of Noah and Lot.

When the Son of Man returns, it will be like it was in Noah's day. In those days, the people enjoyed banquets and parties and weddings right up to the time Noah entered his boat and the flood came and destroyed them all. And the world will be as it was in the days of Lot. People went about their daily business—eating and drinking, buying and selling, farming and building — until the morning Lot left Sodom. Then fire and burning sulfur rained down from heaven and destroyed them all. Yes, it will be 'business as usual' right up to the day when the Son of Man is revealed." (Luke 17:26-31 NLT)

What Jesus is stressing in this scripture is that these two individuals, Noah and Lot, were two men who, although they lived in times when God's judgment was coming upon their world, they believed God and prepared themselves and were not caught unaware. The rest of the people were living life as usual without any regard for God's coming judgment and their end came upon them unexpectantly. Here is the crucial point: when Jesus returns to the earth the Bible says that the world will be in the same condition as it was in the days of Noah and Lot. Most of the people living today are too concerned about living this life and having all the material things this life has to offer. Jesus said:

If you try to hang on to your life, you will lose it. But if you give up your life for my sake and for the sake of the Good News, you will save it. And what do you benefit if you gain the whole world but lose your own soul? Is anything worth more than your soul? (Mark 8:35-37 NLT)

Jesus also said this in Luke 18: "...when the Son of man cometh, shall he find faith on the earth?" *(Luke 18:8)*.

As Christians living in these last days before the 2nd coming of our Lord, we need to make sure that we are ready when He returns. These are not times when we should be casual about our walk with God. We should not be careless how we live our lives. We should not become entangled with this world. In Luke Chapter18, Jesus spoke a parable of an unjust judge to teach His disciples to not lose heart while waiting for His second coming but to be in persistent prayer. He said this because the longer He delayed His coming, the more people would lose faith and fall away. There is no question that Jesus is coming back but when He comes as Jesus said, "Will there be faith in the earth?" Will there be faith in the hearts of men and women to receive Him? Faith in your hearts – faith in my heart!

In the end, the Antichrist will ascend to the world scene on a platform of peace. He will enforce a peace agreement between Israel and the Arabs. This is prophesied in the Book of Daniel, Chapter 9 which was a part of what is generally called the prophecy of Daniel's Seventy Weeks:

Seventy weeks [of years, or 490 years] are decreed upon your people and upon your holy city [Jerusalem], to finish and put an end to transgression, to seal up and make full the measure of sin, to purge away and make expiation and reconciliation for sin, to bring in everlasting righteousness (permanent moral and spiritual rectitude in every area and relation) to seal up vision and prophecy and prophet, and to anoint a Holy of Holies. Know therefore and understand that from the going forth of the commandment to restore and to build Jerusalem until [the coming of] the Anointed One, a Prince, shall be seven weeks [of years] and sixty-two weeks [of years]; it shall be built again with [city] square and moat, but in troublous times. And after the sixty-two weeks [of years] shall the

Anointed One be cut off or killed and shall have nothing [and no one] belonging to [and defending] Him. And the people of the [other] prince who will come will destroy the city and the sanctuary. Its end shall come with a flood; and even to the end there shall be war, and desolations are decreed. And he shall enter into a strong and firm covenant with the many for one week [seven years]. And in the midst of the week he shall cause the sacrifice and offering to cease [for the remaining three and one-half years]; and upon the wing or pinnacle of abominations [shall come] one who makes desolate, until the full determined end is poured out on the desolator. (Daniel 9:24-27 AMP)

Sixty-Nine weeks have already been fulfilled. The seventieth week is known as the Tribulation with the last half of that week (3 ½ years) known as the Great Tribulation. During the time of the Tribulation mankind will become more wicked than ever. At the end of the seventieth week, Jesus Christ will return to put down and destroy all the armies of the world at the Battle of Armageddon. Satan will be bound for one-thousand years and the world will know one-thousand years of peace under the Millennial Reign of Jesus Christ. He will reign as King of Kings and Lord of Lords!

The Importance of Being Ready

There are many warnings that we receive through the words of Jesus and the writings of the Apostles Peter and Paul about how we are to live in these last days. Jesus told His disciples that the Temple in Jerusalem would be thrown down and there would not be one stone laying upon another. He spoke of wars, pestilence, earthquakes, famine, and nations rising up against other nations. He said there would be false prophets deceiving many and because iniquity shall be plentiful the love of many shall grow cold. He said the Gospel would be preached throughout the world and then the end would come. He talked about the Great Tribulation and He said that the tribulation would be so severe that no flesh would be saved, including the elect, if the duration of the days were not shortened. Jesus said in Matthew 24:42,44 that:

Watch therefore: for ye know not what hour your Lord doth come. Therefore be ye also ready: for in such an hour as ye think not the Son of man cometh. (Matthew 24:42,44)

The importance of watching and being ready will especially be necessary because even the true believers do not know exactly when our Lord will come. We may know the season but not the day or hour. The reason Jesus stressed watching and being ready is that once He returns you will have no ability to get ready because His coming will be quick and His judgment will be irreversible. So, Christians need to be prepared for His coming at any time. The Apostles warned with similar cautions as those of Jesus.

Besides this you know what [a critical] hour this is, how it is high time now for you to wake up out of your sleep (rouse to reality). For salvation (final deliverance) is nearer to us now than when we first believed (adhered to, trusted in, and relied on Christ, the Messiah). (Romans 13:11 AMP)

This is all the more urgent, for you know how late it is; time is running out. Wake up, for our salvation is nearer now than when we first believed. (Romans 13:11 NLT)

Paul was attempting to alert the believers in his day and also in ours that we should wake up because our salvation is nearer this day than when we were first Born Again. For that reason and because the Lord could come at any time, we should conduct ourselves honorably and not be drunk, participating in wild parties. We should refrain from immorality and sexual promiscuity. We should cast off all the works of darkness and we should put on the Lord Jesus Christ. We should make no provision for gratifying the lust of our flesh or think about ways to indulge our evil desires.

In 1 Thessalonians 5, Paul was speaking about the Day of the Lord, which is the day when Jesus will return to the earth. He said that He will come very unexpectantly and suddenly to those living in the world and unprepared for His coming. When He comes, He will come as a thief and for them there will be no escape *(1 Thessalonians 5:2-5)*. But for the Born-Again Christians who continue to walk in His ways, He will not come as a thief, for we will be awaiting His coming. For this reason, Paul warns us to be on our guard, and not be asleep as the others are. We should be alert and clear-headed and this way we will not miss His return.

The Apostle Peter, writing in his last epistle *(2 Peter)*, tells us that in the last days many scoffers would come. According to the Life Application Bible Commentary, scoffers are:

Those who base their lives and teaching on sinful desires, those who ignore the teaching of Christ's return and coming judgment, and those who base their view of God's role in history on outward circumstances, economic trends, and international events while neglecting the teachings of Scripture. [7]

I'm quite sure that any Christian living today who has tried to share Jesus Christ with others has met with some scoffers and mockers. Peter, in his epistle wrote that they would mock and say, "Where is the promise of His coming?" We have heard this just like our ancestors did.

The scoffers based their arguments on the fact that since our ancestors died, all things continue as they were from the beginning of creation. 'Nothing has really changed, so why think that it ever will?'...Therefore they scoffed at teachings about a Second Coming and the end of the world. [8]

Likewise, the Apostle Paul wrote to Timothy:

> *For the time will come when they will not endure sound doctrine; but after their own lusts shall they heap to themselves teachers, having itching ears; And they shall turn away their ears from the truth, and shall be turned unto fables. (2 Timothy 4:3-4)*

But make no mistake about it; there will be a coming judgment when Jesus returns to silence all the mockers, scoffers, and all false teachers. What they don't understand is that Jesus' delay is for their benefit and ours. He is so unwilling to see anyone perish in the flames of hell that He delays His coming waiting with such longsuffering for that last soul to repent and to be born into His Kingdom. Peter explains that it may take a long time in coming, but one day it will come and when it does it will come like a thief in the night for those who are not ready, waiting, and watching for His return. When it comes it will be a day of judgment. As Peter writes:

> *But the day of the Lord will come as a thief in the night; in the which the heavens shall pass away with a great noise, and the elements shall melt with fervent heat, the earth also and the works that are therein shall be burned up. (2 Peter 3:10)*

> *But the day of the Lord will come like a thief, and then the heavens will vanish (pass away) with a thunderous crash, and the [material] elements [of the universe] will be dissolved with fire, and the earth and the works that are upon it will be burned up. (2 Peter 3:10 AMP)*

This is speaking of a time of great upheaval upon the earth and of cosmic destruction in the heavenlies. Even Jesus said, "That the stars would fall from the sky, and the heavenly bodies would not give their light" *(Matthew 24 NIV)*. Everything in the earth will one day be burned up. We can only imagine what this will be like. All the great edifices erected throughout history will disappear. All men's possessions, their wealth, silver, gold, jewelry, clothing, cars, trucks, etc. will perish in the flames of destruction. Everything people trust in is going to go up in flames. All of their hopes, dreams, and plans will burn with an intense heat. Since this will definitely happen, what kind of persons ought we to be? What kind of lives should we be living?

Living An Abundant Life

We should live out these days of our lives preaching and sharing the good news of the Gospel of Our Lord Jesus Christ. We should be so thankful for what God has done for us. We should live our lives so that they please God and give Him praise all of our days. For God had reconciled us to Himself. We who were sinners; we who were the enemies of God; we who were of hostile attitude of mind and worthy of nothing but death, has God reconciled and restored to favor with Himself. Now every Born Again Apostolic Christian no longer has the pall of death hanging over Him but we have a promise of a new and better life, for our old life has passed away, and all things are new.

> *Therefore, if any man be in Christ, he is a new creature: old things are passed away; behold, all things are become new. (2 Corinthians 5:17)*

And now our new life on earth consists of being an ambassador for Jesus Christ, helping to bring to the world the ministry of reconciliation. Living this life on earth with the Holy Ghost within us is indeed a good life. It's much better than the life we previously had been living. Jesus said He came to give us a more abundant life: "...I am come that they might have life, and that they might have it more abundantly."

Jesus wants us to have an abundant life. I truly believe that this abundant life that Jesus promised for us will begin when we give ourselves to Christ. The Complete Word Study of the New Testament says this about the word "abundant:"

> *It has a general meaning of "superabundance" as in John 10:10. But by implication in a comparative sense it can also take on the meaning of "more abundant, excellent, or better.* [9]

Now when we are speaking of a superabundant life my thoughts go directly to what it will be like to live in eternity with Jesus. That to me would be an abundant life! However, I do believe that we are privileged to live lives on earth that far surpass the lives of ordinary people. Once we are born again, we step into an abundant life with Christ right here on earth. The Life Application Bible Commentary on John says this:

Abundance of life points to depth of living now and length of living in eternity. It is not only life as good as it could be, but also life beyond what we could imagine. [10]

I have always said that this life we live in Christ is the best life we could ever live on earth. That is because Jesus is with us always. However, it is not a life without trouble for Jesus told us that in this life we would have tribulation (*John 16:33*). We are not immune to trouble once we come into God's Kingdom. Although God takes care of us, He doesn't shield us from everything. These can be trials, tribulations, troubles, sicknesses, diseases, or hospitalizations. We can be involved in accidents; we can be a victim of a crime; we can have our cars or houses broken into. We will eventually suffer the loss of someone very near and dear to us. These trials and tribulations have a way of changing us, making us into what God would have us to be. Even today there are Christians living in certain areas where it is dangerous for their Christian faith to be uncovered. If exposed, many times they are martyred. Yes, in this world we will have tribulation but Jesus also said, "be of good cheer for I have overcome the world" (*John 16:33*). Right here and now, Jesus gives us love, peace, joy, forgiveness, comfort, and a blessed assurance that there is something so enormously magnificent beyond the grave.

As wonderful as this blessed life we live in Christ here on earth is, there is going to be no comparison to what life will be like once we step into eternity. We can only imagine what God has prepared for us there. Jesus told His Apostles in John Chapter 14 that He was going away to prepare a place for them and He said that He would come back for them and receive them unto Himself. I believe that was meant for all of those who have obeyed God's Word and have been Born Again of water and the Spirit. Jesus is coming back to take His faithful followers, His loving believers, home. We call this the "catching away" of the Church and some refer to it as the Rapture. This is the first resurrection (*Revelation 20:5*). We should all desire to take part in this resurrection because this is a resurrection unto life eternal. There will be another resurrection but that one will be to stand before God at His Great White Throne (*Revelation 20:11-14*). As one stands before God there, God will judge the individual out of the books, which we believe will be His Word (*John 14:48*). There will also be a Book of Life there and if the individual's name is not found written in that book, he will be cast into the Lake of Fire for all eternity (*Revelation 20:15*). This is known as the second death! I know that sounds quite frightening, but it is the Word of God. That is the final judgment for all who reject the Lord's plan of salvation. Jesus died and shed His blood on Calvary so that we would not end up in the Lake of Fire for eternity. He told Nicodemus:

> *Verily, verily, I say unto thee, Except a man be born of water and of the Spirit, he CANNOT enter into the kingdom of God. (John 3:5)*

It's Your Choice

What is the meaning of this life? Is it meant to get all that you can and be the best you can be? Are we to fill up our impulses and indulge ourselves in everything we desire? Do we always have to please ourselves? What is the purpose of this life? In the Bible, King Solomon was the wisest man ever known. God granted him such great wisdom. In his later years Solomon drifted away from the Lord. In the Book of Ecclesiastes, Solomon writes about all the great things he had done. He tells us that whatever he desired in life he kept not from himself. He had great wealth, lands, beautiful gardens, the choicest of foods and drink, many servants, and quite a few girls in the harem (*700 wives and 300 concubines*). You would think that he would have been the happiest man ever. In fact, he was miserable. He looked at all his hands had made and all he had gathered of this world's goods and he said it was all vanity and vexation of spirit, and there was no profit under the sun.

At the end of the book, Solomon wrote these words most likely reflecting back on his life and realizing that no matter what he accumulated in this life, in the end his body will go back to the dust it came from and his spirit will go back to God who gave it. And what would be said of his life and even more important, what will be the place where he spends eternity? That is why he summed up life and gave us his wise conclusion on the matter when he said:

Let us hear the conclusion of the whole matter: Fear God, and keep his commandments: for this is the whole duty of man. For God shall bring every work into judgment, with every secret thing, whether it be good, or whether it be evil. (Ecclesiastes 12:13-14)

Jesus warns us:

And what do you benefit if you gain the whole world but lose your own soul? Is anything worth more than your soul? (Matthew 16:26 [NIV])

For what will it profit a man if he gains the whole world and forfeits his life [his blessed life in the kingdom of God]? Or what would a man give as an exchange for his [blessed] life [in the kingdom of God]? (Matthew 16:26 AMP)

So where do we all stand? There are few scriptures that do let us know what will happen to us in the future. In Ecclesiastes 3: 2, it says: "A time to be born, and a time to die..." Hebrews 9:27 also discusses this: "And as it is appointed unto men once to die, but after this the judgment." These scriptures teach us that our lives will not be forever here on this earth. We must be mindful that this world is not, nor should we make it, our home. God has chosen a better place. In the introduction to his book, *One Minute After You Die*, Erwin Lutzer writes:

> *One minute after you slip behind the parted curtain, you will either be enjoying a personal welcome from Christ or catching your first glimpse of gloom as you have never known it. Either way, your future will be irrevocably fixed and eternally unchangeable.* [11]

What a somber way to introduce a book! However, the fact remains that what Mr. Lutzer stated is probably the absolute truth. Once we die, we will either be with the Lord in glory or else we will be without the Lord in suffering. There is no intermediate place. And Jesus adds His Words to the gloomy side of the story. He tells us that there will be more people who choose to spend eternity in the darkness of the Lake of Fire than those who choose to live with Jesus in heaven.

> *Enter ye in at the strait gate: for wide is the gate, and broad is the way, that leadeth to destruction, and MANY there be which go in thereat: Because strait is the gate, and narrow is the way, which leadeth unto life, and FEW there be that find it. (Matthew 7:13-14)*

Final Thoughts

Have you chosen the way you will go? Will you be one of the few? Truthfully the choice is yours to make. If you will choose to give up this sinful life you live now and make that 180 degree turn in repentance, God will put His Holy Spirit in you and you will be on the road to eternal life. If you have already made that choice, what a glorious future awaits you. However, if you have not made your choice to walk that narrow road that leads to eternal life with Jesus, this would be a great time to make up your mind to do so.

12
GOD'S GLORIOUS KINGDOM

Does the Bible tell us about God's Heavenly Kingdom? I began my introduction to this book with the word "Heaven," and I am going to end this book on the same note. Heaven is where I want to be. Heaven is where you should want to be. Knowing how great God is and has been throughout our lifetime we can just imagine how awesome it will be to enter into that Glorious Kingdom of God!

What Will Heaven Be Like?

But can we know what life in the Kingdom will be like? How will we live? What will we do? Does the Bible tell us? Paul did write in one of his epistles that:

Yet when I am among mature believers, I do speak with words of wisdom, but not the kind of wisdom that belongs to this world or to the rulers of this world, who are soon forgotten. No, the wisdom we speak of is the mystery of God—his plan that was previously hidden, even though he made it for our ultimate glory before the world began. But the rulers of this world have not understood it; if they had, they would not have crucified our glorious Lord. That is what the Scriptures mean when they say, No eye has seen, no ear has heard, and no mind has imagined what God has prepared for those who love him. But it was to us that God revealed these things by his Spirit. For his Spirit searches out everything and shows us God's deep secrets. (1 Corinthians 2:6-11 NLT)

The secret things belong unto the LORD our God: but those things which are revealed belong unto us and to our children for ever, that we may do all the words of this law. (Deuteronomy 29:29)

Randy Alcorn writes this about the above scriptures:

We should accept that many things about heaven are secret, and that God has countless surprises in store for us. But as for the things God has revealed to us about heaven, these things belong to us and to our children. It's critically important that we study and understand them. That is precisely why God has revealed them to us! [1]

So, what does happen when we die? Of course, we don't know everything but some things can be understood. We will most likely be met by angels at the door as we enter from life on earth. We will realize that we are no longer on earth but we have entered a different realm or dimension. We are in heaven! Or maybe we are in the other place? I hope that is not the case with you. We will come face-to-face with Our Lord Jesus Christ. What a wonderful and glorious meeting that will be. I just cannot imagine how amazing it will be to see Him. He is the reason heaven will be heaven. We will then begin to meet with all the rest of the brethren in Christ who have died before us. We will be reunited with family members, friends, and we will meet people we never knew in life but had read about in the Bible. Can you imagine meeting the Apostle Paul and talking with Him? Peter? Moses or Abraham? That should keep us busy for a while.

What will we be doing in heaven? We probably will not be disembodied spirits just floating around on the clouds in the universe. Now that would be a waste of time. However, I do believe that God has something great in store for all of us. But first things first. We will worship Him!

Praise and Worship will be our first order of service to God in heaven. We will give God praise and we will worship Him always. That doesn't mean that we do nothing else, but God is worthy to receive such glorious praise. After all, if it wasn't that He died for us and gave us the grace to be saved we wouldn't be in heaven. Just look at Revelation 4 and 5. He is worthy!

> *And when those beasts give glory and honour and thanks to him that sat on the throne, who liveth for ever and ever, The four and twenty elders fall down before him that sat on the throne, and worship him that liveth for ever and ever, and cast their crowns before the throne, saying, Thou art worthy, O Lord, to receive glory and honour and power: for thou hast created all things, and for thy pleasure they are and were created. (Revelation 4:9-11)*

> *And when he had taken the book, the four beasts and four and twenty elders fell down before the Lamb, having every one of them harps, and golden vials full of odours, which are the prayers of saints. And they sung a new song, saying, Thou art worthy to take the book, and to open the seals thereof: for thou wast slain, and hast redeemed us to God by thy blood out of every kindred, and tongue, and people, and nation; And hast made us unto our God kings and priests: and we shall reign on the earth. And I beheld, and I heard the voice of many angels round about the throne and the beasts and the elders: and the number of them was ten thousand times ten thousand, and thousands of thousands; Saying with a loud voice, Worthy is the Lamb that was slain to receive power, and riches, and wisdom, and strength, and honour, and glory, and blessing. And every creature which is in heaven, and on the earth, and under the earth, and such as are in the sea, and all that are in them, heard I saying, Blessing, and honour, and glory, and power, be unto him that sitteth upon the throne, and unto the Lamb for ever and ever.*

> *And the four beasts said, Amen. And the four and twenty elders fell down and worshipped him that liveth for ever and ever. (Revelation 5:8-14)*

We will be able to worship Him without any human restraints. Have you ever been in a worship service where the presence of God filled the place and you were able to worship Him for a good period of time but then your body started to cause you to lose focus? That will not happen in heaven. We will worship Him without any earthly limitations.

> *...and his servants shall serve him: And they shall see his face; and his name shall be in their foreheads. (Revelation 22:3-4)*

Then we will serve Him. Again, this is something that we did when we lived on earth. Erwin Lutzer writes about this:

> *Though worship shall occupy much of our time in heaven, we will also be assigned responsibilities commensurate with the faithfulness we displayed here on earth.* [2]

In Randy Alcorn's book, "Heaven", he writes this concerning serving God:

> *Service is a reward, not a punishment. This idea is foreign to people who disliked their work and only put up with it until retirement. We think that faithful work should be rewarded by a vacation for the rest of our lives. But God offers us something very different: more work, more responsibilities, increased opportunities, along with greater abilities, resources, wisdom, and empowerment. We will have sharp minds, strong bodies, clear purpose, and unabated joy. The more we serve Christ now, the greater our capacity will be to serve him in heaven.* [3]

Thinking about all that God will give us to do should excite us. We should desire to serve God now and be faithful in the responsibilities that we have been given on earth. One thing seems obvious, we will not be bored.

A Completely Different Life

While it is true that our soul lives on and never dies, that doesn't mean that our life or our surroundings do not change. Living eternally in heaven with Jesus will be a completely different life than what we are used to. And a much better one. The Book of Revelation gives us some great clues to what awaits us in heaven.

1. We will not hunger or thirst anymore nor ever be scorched by the heat of the sun.

For this reason they are [now] before the [very] throne of God and serve Him day and night in His sanctuary (temple); and He Who is sitting upon the throne will protect and spread His tabernacle over and shelter them with His presence. They shall hunger no more, neither thirst any more; neither shall the sun smite them, nor any scorching heat. (Revelation 7:15:16)

2. There will be no crying there. God will wipe away all our tears from our eyes.

For the Lamb which is in the midst of the throne shall feed them, and shall lead them unto living fountains of waters: and God shall wipe away all tears from their eyes. (Revelation 7:17)

3. Besides there being no more crying, there will also be no more death, or sorrow, or pain. Now that is glorious news!

And God shall wipe away all tears from their eyes; and there shall be no more death, neither sorrow, nor crying, neither shall there be any more pain: for the former things are passed away. (Revelation 21:4)

Can you imagine life without bad news? Just turn on any news channel today and that's about all we hear, bad news. We won't have to worry about accidents, or crimes committed against good citizens. We won't have sorrow because there will be no more death. And then we will have a body that is free from all pain! Anyone who has reached the age of 40 is starting to feel the decline of his/her body. The older you get the worse it gets. But we could live one million years in eternity and we will feel no pain! To God be the Glory!

4. We will inherit all things

He that overcometh shall inherit all things; and I will be his God, and he shall be my son. (Revelation 21:7)

The Bible also says this:

And since we are his children, we are his heirs. In fact, together with Christ we are heirs of God's glory. But if we are to share his glory, we must also share his suffering. (Romans 8:17 NLT)

Do we get the picture here? Simply because God loves us with such a selfless love, we become His children. And as His children we are heirs of God and joint heirs with Christ. Everything belongs to God and He has given all to Jesus Christ. That means we share with Christ all that belongs to Him. That is unbelievable!

5. There will be no need for the sun or moon because the Glory of God will be the light. There will also be no night there so we won't need any type of artificial light.

> *I saw no temple in the city, for the Lord God Omnipotent [Himself] and the Lamb [Himself] are its temple. And the city has no need of the sun nor of the moon to give light to it, for the splendor and radiance (glory) of God illuminate it, and the Lamb is its lamp. (Revelation 21:22-23 AMP)*
>
> *And there shall be no night there; and they need no candle, neither light of the sun; for the Lord God giveth them light: and they shall reign for ever and ever. (Revelation 22:5)*

6. Nothing sinful, wicked, or defiling and no abomination will ever enter there.

> *But the fearful, and unbelieving, and the abominable, and murderers, and whoremongers, and sorcerers, and idolaters, and all liars, shall have their part in the lake which burneth with fire and brimstone: which is the second death... And there shall in no wise enter into it any thing that defileth, neither whatsoever worketh abomination, or maketh a lie: but they which are written in the Lamb's book of life. (Revelation 21:8,27)*

Final Thoughts

Throughout this book I have been trying to show anyone who will open his heart and mind to the scripture, the way into the Kingdom of God/Heaven. I am not trying to be arrogant, argumentative, or offensive though I know that sometimes it may sound that way. You certainly have a right to disagree with me, and if you do, I respect your position. I ask you to please read all of the scriptural references and pray over them. Meditate upon them and let God speak to your heart.

It doesn't matter what you have already experienced in God. That is all good. I'm not trying to take anything away from you, but I hope and pray that God will add to your experience, whatever that may be. Maybe this book can lead you into a more perfect way into God's Kingdom.

There is one thing that is a foregone conclusion in this life. If you are reading this book, it is an absolute fact that someday you will die.

Most people dread the thought of death and I guess the mystery of what lies beyond the grave frightens us. But we should be afraid if we are to die without ever having been born again. For the Born-Again Christian there is hope beyond this life and death is not an end, death is not a curse, and death is not a finality. Death is just a door that will lead us into the Glorious Kingdom of God!

If you have never given your life to Jesus Christ or if you are interested in an even deeper experience with Jesus, please contact me through my email address: joe.thykingdomcome@gmail.com, and I will help you find your way into the Kingdom of God.

ACKNOWLEDGMENTS

First of all, to be sitting here writing an acknowledgments page to a book is something I never thought I would do. Writing a book has been something I wanted to do since the moment the Lord filled me with the Holy Ghost. I tried then but couldn't get past the first chapter.

This present writing came about as I was thinking of putting some short lessons on YouTube and was told by some people, "Why don't you write a book instead?" After some serious thought I figured that I would give it a try. Well, here it is. Seriously though, this task could not have been accomplished without the help of some very special people.

First, I give the honor and praise to my God and Savior Jesus Christ, who motivated me all along the way. Without His help I could never have completed this book.

My thanks to Mary Unz who painstakingly edited my drafts many times over and gave me some valuable help in other ways. She always encouraged me by saying how much see enjoyed reading each chapter.

I thank my current pastor Harold Linder for lending me some of his books that I used greatly in studying to write this book. He also gave me time off from church ministry to allow me to finish this writing.

I give thanks to my former pastors, Gerald Morris and Doug Davis Jr. These men have molded and shaped my life according to the Word of God. I so appreciate them being willing to write the forewords for this book.

I give honor to my former pastor and friend, the late Victor M. Melendez, for mentoring me for four years. I have to believe that walking alongside him helped me to experience some things I would never have experienced. I miss him so much.

I am grateful to Julia, Cassandra, Elizabeth, Lou, and Bob for allowing me to retell their miraculous stories in order to give glory to God.

I express my thanks to Janice Broyles of Late November Publishing, who worked with me through the manuscript and helped to inspire me not only to achieve my goal to finish this book but also to see it published. She also gave me much help in arranging the content of the writing and offered valuable insights in the editing process.

Finally, I pay tribute to my loving and faithful wife Barbara, who kept reading over my drafts and helped me edit them to rephrase and in some cases rewrite some of the content of this book. She also helped me to remember some of the personal stories that are written in this book. Thank you, babe, for giving me all the time I needed to accomplish this work. You have been my constant inspiration and I could not have done it without you.

END NOTES

THE KINGDOM OF GOD

1. "Thy Kingdom Come" by J.Dwight Pentecost, Kregel Publications, page 11
2. "The Gospel of the Kingdom" by George Eldon Ladd, William B. Eerdmans Publishing Co. p 11
3. "The Complete Bible Library New Testament Commentary, Vol 1., Empowered Life Publishers, p787
4. "Thy Kingdom Come" by J Dwight Pentecost, Kregel Pub, page 32.
5. Ibid, p 35.
6. "The Complete Word Study Dictionary of the Old Testament", AMG Publishers Warren Baker, D.R.E. and Eugene Carpenter, Ph.D, Page 755
7. "Thy Kingdom Come" Kregel Publications, by J Dwight Pentecost, page 58
8. Ibid, page 59

9. "The MacArthur New Testament Commentary on Matthew 1-7", Moody Publishers, pages 54-55.
10. Strongs Index (Greek) No. 1448.
11. "Thomas Coke's Commentary on the whole Bible online on Matt 4:17", by Thomas Coke LL.D, Vol 5.
12. "The New Birth" Word Aflame Press, David K. Bernard, p104
13. "John, The Gospel That Had to be Written", by Fred E. Kinzie, Word Aflame Press 1995, page 67.

YE SHALL RECEIVE POWER

1. "Christ Centered Exposition Commentary" by Tony Merida, p 5. B&H Publishing Group, Nashville TN
2. "Life Application Study Bible", Tyndale House Publishers, p.2228
3. "The Gospel According to Luke", William B. Eerdmans Publishing, by James R. Edwards, p. 7
4. "New American Commentary, Gospel of Luke", B&H Publishing Group, page 65
5. Precept Austin website: https://www.preceptaustin.org/acts-1-commentary#1:1
6. "The Complete Bible Library New Testament Commentary, Vol 1., Empowered Life Publishers, p.607
7. Precept Austin website: https://www.preceptaustin.org/acts-1-commentary#1:1
8. Barnes, Albert. "Commentary on Acts 1:1". "Barnes' Notes on the Whole Bible".
9. "Life Application Bible Commentary", Tyndale House Publishers, ch 1, vss 1-2 page 1-2.
10. "Life Application Bible Commentary", Tyndale House Publishers, ch 1, vs 2, page 2.

11. "Life Application Bible Commentary", Tyndale House Publishers, ch 1, vs 4-5, page 5.
12. "The Tony Evans Bible Commentary", Holman Bible Publishers, by Tony Evans, p11
13. "Christ Centered Exposition Commentary" by Tony Merida, p 1132. B&H Publishing Group, Nashville TN

WHAT MEANETH THIS?

1. "Wycliffe Bible Dictionary", Hendrickson Publishers, page 1306-1307
2. "Acts: An Expositional Commentary", Reformation Trust Publishing, 2019 by R.C. Sproul, pages 20-21
3. "The Complete Word Study Dictionary", New Testament #3661, page 1040
4. "The Complete Bible Library", New Testament Commentary, Vol 2, page 59
5. "The MacArthur New Testament Commentary, 1 Corinthians", Moody Publishers, p. 362
6. "Acts: An Expositional Commentary", Reformation Trust Publishing, 2019 by R.C. Sproul, page 23.
7. "What Meaneth This", Gospel Publishing House, by Carl Brumback, pp.89-92, 237
8. Passage taken from Bethel United Pentecostal Church's Discipleship Course, Lesson on Speaking With Tongues, p 81
9. "Acts: Baker Exegetical Commentary on the New Testament", Baker Academic a division of Baker Publishing Group, by Darrell L. Bock, p106.

PETER'S FIRST GOSPEL SERMON

1. "The NIV New Application Commentary: Acts", Zondervan Pub Co. by Ajith Fernando
2. "Acts", Baker Publishing Co. by Darrell Bock, p112
3. "Christ Centered Exposition Commentary" by Tony Merida, p 31. B&H Publishing Group, Nashville TN
4. "Decision Magazine", October 2022 edition, p29
5. "The Acts of the Apostles, A Socio-Rhetorical Commentary", Eerdmans Publishing Co, by Ben Witherington, p.139
6. "Acts of the Apostles, A Socio-Rhetorical Commentary", Eerdmans Publishing Co. by Ben Witherington, pp 154-155
7. "The NIV Application Commentary, Acts" Zondervan Publishing, by Ajith Fernandez, p. 291
8. "Ephesians, A Commentary, The Bride's Pearl, Word Aflame Press, by Brian Kinsey, p135
9. "Pentecostal Life Magazine", Feb 2022 issue, "Cheap Grace" an article written by Scott Graham, General Secretary-Treasurer of the United Pentecostal Church Intl.

THEY CONTINUED

1. "The Story of God Bible Commentary", Zondervan publishing, Dean printer, p 82. #1
2. "Pulpit Commentary" online on Acts 2:42
3. "Preacher Outline and Sermon Bible", Acts of the Apostles, Alpha-Omega Ministries Inc, p. 40, deeper study #3.
4. "William Burkitt's" online notes on 1 Corinthians 10:16
5. "Acts A Logion Press Commentary", Gospel Publishing House, by Stanley M. Horton, p 84.
6. "Mounce Complete Expository Dictionary of Old and New Testament Words", Zondervan, Grand Rapids, Mi, page 82.

END NOTES

7. "Life Application Bible Commentary", 1 & 2 Corinthians, Tyndale, page 159 on Chapter 11:20-21
8. "The New American Commentary", Acts Vol 26, NIV, B&H Publishing Group, page 122
9. "Christ-Centered Exposition, Exalting Jesus in Acts", by Tony Merida, B&H Publishing Co. page 39

BEFORE THE JEWISH COUNCIL

1. "The Story of God Bible Commentary", Acts, Zondervan, p. 95
2. Swordsearcher 8.3 Online Bible Program on Acts 3:19, Strongs Greek Dictionary, G3340
3. Ibid, Strongs Greek Dictionary, G1813
4. "Christ-Centered Exposition, Exalting Jesus in Acts by Tony Merida, B&H Publishing Co. page 53-54.
5. "The New Birth" by David Bernard, Word Aflame Publishing, p73
6. "Acts, A Logion Press Commentary" by Stanley Horton, Gospel Publishing House, pg 95
7. "Precept Austin" website: The Acts of the Apostles, Section I: Acts 1 to 7, an expositional study by Warren Doud, Lesson 9: Acts 3:17-26.
8. Precept Austin website, Acts Ch. 3 under "Times of Refreshing" by Kenneth Gangel.
9. Acts, A Logion Press Commentary by Stanley Horton, Gospel Publishing House, pg 95
10. "The Story of God Bible Commentary", Acts, Zondervan, Dean Pinter, p103.
11. "The Complete Word Study Dictionary", New Testament, by Spiros Zodhiates, AMG Int'l, page 1503.
12. "Acts, A Logion Press Commentary" by Stanley Horton, Gospel Publishing House, pg 102.

13. "The Story of God Bible Commentary, Acts" by Dean Pinter, Zondervan, p113.
14. "The Life Application Bible Commentary", John, Tyndale House Publishers, Inc, page 10.
15. "The Complete Word Study Dictionary", New Testament, by Spiros Zodhiates, AMG Int'l, page 400.
16. Wikipedia on "Baptism in the Name of Jesus"
17. "The New Birth" by David Bernard, Word Aflame Publishing, p83

ON TO THE GENTILES

1. "Thehistoryofkeys.com," Website
2. "The New Birth" by David Bernard, Word Aflame Press, www.pentecostalpublishing.com, pp. 72-73
3. "Zondervan Illustrated Bible Backgrounds Commentary", Vol 2, Clinton Arnold General Editor, page 301
4. Ibid page 303.
5. "Acts, A Logion Press Commentary" by Stanley M. Horton, Gospel Publishing Co. p196.
6. "Acts" A Baker Exegetical Commentary, Baker Publishing Group, by Darrell Bock p385.
7. "The Baker Illustrated Bible Background Commentary", Baker Books, Editors J. Scott Duvall and J. Daniel Hays, page 1027
8. "The Story of God Commentary", Zondervan Pub, Dean Pinter, page 253.
9. "Zondervan Illustrated Bible Backgrounds Commentary", Vol 2, Clinton Arnold General Editor, page 307.
10. "Acts, A Logion Press Commentary", Gospel Publishing Co. pps 198-199
11. "The Complete Word Study Dictionary of the NT" by Spiros Zodhiates Th.D. page 553 Gr Word 1611 (II).

12. "Zondervan Illustrated Bible Backgrounds Commentary", Vol 2, Clinton Arnold General Editor, page 307
13. "The Literal Word", Acts 1, Treasure House, Shippensburg, Pa, M.D. Treece page 347
14. "Acts, A Logion Press Commentary", Gospel Publishing Co. pps 194-195
15. "Zondervan Illustrated Bible Backgrounds Commentary", Vol 2, Clinton Arnold General Editor, page 310
16. "Acts, A Logion Press Commentary", by Stanley M. Horton, Gospel Publishing Co. p 206.
17. "The Acts of the Apostles" A Socio-Rhetorical Commentary, William B. Eerdmans Pub Co. by Ben Witherington III, p360
18. "Spirit and Power:Foundations of Pentecostal Experience William W. Menzies and Robert P. Menzies, Grand Rapids: Zondervan Publishing House, 2000, p 129.
19. "The Acts of the Apostles" A Socio-Rhetorical Commentary, William B. Eerdmans Pub Co. by Ben Witherington III, p364
20. "Acts, A Logion Press Commentary" by Stanley M. Horton, Gospel Publishing Co. p. 211

AN ABOUT FACE

1. "Acts" Baker Exegetical Commentary, Baker Pub Group, by Darrell L.Bock, p.314
2. "The Story of God Bible Commentary", Acts, Zondervan Publishing, by Dean Pinter, p 194.
3. "Josh McDowell A Cru Ministry", online at www.Josh.org/ddl-video/saul-of-tarsus.
4. "Precept Austin website", Acts Ch 9, J.R. Miller, Acts 9:1-30 - The Conversion of Saul
5. "Acts" Baker Exegetical Commentary, Baker Publishing Group, by Darrell L. Bock, p 319.

6. "Story of God Bible Commentary" Acts, Zondervan Pub, by Dean Pinter, p 223.
7. "Acts" A Logion Press Commentary", Gospel Pub House, Stanley L Horton, p 180.
8. " Story of God Bible Commentary Acts", Zondervan Pub, by Dean Pinter, p 225.
9. "Christ-Centered Exposition, Exalting Jesus in Acts", B&H Pub Group, by Tony Merida, p. 134
10. "Acts, New Application Bible Commentary", Zondervan Pub Co. by Ajith Fernando, p. 300.
11. "Acts, A Logion Commentary", Gospel Pub House, by Stanley L. Horton, pp 185
12. "The Complete Word Study Dictionary" AMG Int'l Pub, Greek Word #3619, p 1031.
13. "The Complete Word Study Dictionary" AMG Int'l Pub, Greek Word #2112, p 673.
14. "Acts, New Application Bible Commentary", Zondervan Pub Co. by Ajith Fernando, p. 505.
15. "Story of God Bible Commentary" Acts, Zondervan Pub, by Dean Pinter, p 435.

THE GOSPEL TO SAMARIA

1. "Acts, A Logion Press Commentary", Gospel Pub Co, by Stanley Horton, p159
2. "The New Application Commentary, Acts", Zondervan Pub, by Ajith Fernando, p.263-264
3. "The Wiersbe Study Bible", Thomas Nelson Pub, notes on page 1607 vs 8:1-3)
4. Wikipedia on Samaria
5. "Story of God Bible Commentary, Acts", Zondervan Pub Co., by Dean Pinter, p202

6. "Acts" Baker Exegetical Commentary on the New Testament, Baker Academic, by Darrell Bock pg 329.
7. "Ibid p. 328
8. "Thy Kingdom Come", Kregel Publications, by J. Dwight Pentecost, pp 277
9. "Acts, A Logion Press Commentary", Gospel Pub Co, by Stanley Horton, p164
10. "Story of God Bible Commentary, Acts", Zondervan Pub Co., by Dean Pinter, p204
11. "Exalting Jesus in Acts", A Christ Centered Exposition B&H Publishing Group, by Tony Merida, pg 117
12. "The New Birth" Word Aflame Press, by David Bernard p 205
13. "Story of God Bible Commentary, Acts", Zondervan Pub Co., by Dean Pinter, p212
14. "Acts, A Logion Press Commentary", Gospel Publishing House, by Stanley M. Horton, p174
15. "Story of God Bible Commentary, Acts", Zondervan Pub Co., by Dean Pinter, p378
16. "The NLT Life Application Study Bible", Tyndale House Publishers, p 2496
17. "Acts of the Apostles, a Socio-Rhetorical Commentary, Wm. B. Eerdmans Publishing Co, by Ben Witherington III, pg 493
18. "The New Birth", Word Aflame Press, by Dr. David Bernard, p.213.

CHAPTER TWENTY-NINE

1. "Conquest Through Prayer", Word Aflame Press, by Denzil Holman, p19
2. "E.M. Bounds on Prayer", Whitaker House Publishing, by E.M. Bounds, pp. 11,13.

3. "The John MacArthur New Testament Commentary, Hebrews", Moody Publishers, p.287
4. "The Message of Romans" by David K. Bernard, Word Aflame Press, p.265
5. "Living By Faith" by Daniel L. Seagraves, Published by Daniel L , Seagraves, p. 247
6. "Practical Holiness, A Second Look", Word Aflame Press, by David K. Bernard, p.32-33.
7. "Ephesians, A Commentary, The Bride's Pearl", Word Aflame Press, pp 217.
8. Ibid p 218
9. "The MacArthur New Testament Commentary, First Corinthians, Moody Publishers, pp.211 and 213
10. "The Life Application Bible Commentary, 1st & 2nd Corinthians," Tyndale House Publishers, p.128

THE END OF THE AGE

1. "The Genesis Record", Baker Book House, by Henry Morris, p.252
2. Ibid p 252
3. "Life Death and the End of the World", Apostolic Teaching Resources, by David S. Norris, p.63-64.
4. "Genesis Volume 1", An Expositional Commentary, Creation and the Fall (Gen 1-11), Baker Books, by James Montgomery Boice, p. 423
5. "The Genesis Record", Baker Book House, by Henry Morris, p.265
6. Website Endtime.com
7. "The Life Application Bible Commentary 1 & 2 Peter/Jude", Tyndale House Publishers, p. 201
8. Ibid pp. 202-203

9. "The Complete Word Study Dictionary of the New Tesatament", AMG Publishers, Spiros Zodhiates Td.D, Strongs # 4053, p.1151-1152
10. "The Life Application Bible Commentary John", Tyndale House Publishers, p. 208.
11. "One Minute After You Die", Moody Publishers, by Erwin W. Lutzer, p.9

GOD'S GLORIOUS KINGDOM

1. "Heaven", Tyndale House Publishers, by Randy Alcorn, p. 19
2. "One Minute After You Die", Moody Publishers, by Erwin W. Lutzer, p.88
3. "Heaven", Tyndale House Publishers, by Randy Alcorn, p. 234

Thank you for purchasing this book!
Read more from Joseph Ferragamo Sr. at his website & blog:
www.josephferragamo.com

www.ingramcontent.com/pod-product-compliance
Lightning Source LLC
Chambersburg PA
CBHW070655120526
44590CB00013BA/970